⟨◁ W9-DFZ-988

Bible Teaching

FOR FOUR'S AND FIVE'S

Melva Cook

Convention Press

NASHVILLE   TENNESSEE

Code Number: Church Study Course
This book is number 1757 in category 17, section
for Adults and Young People.

Library of Congress Catalog Card Number: 60-10783
Printed in the United States of America
7.5 F 63 R.R.D.

About the Author

MELVA COOK was born and reared in Texas. She received the Bachelor of Science degree from North Texas State College, with a major in kindergarten-primary education, and took additional work in elementary education at Southwestern Baptist Theological Seminary.

Miss Cook served as elementary secretary with the Sunday School Department of the Baptist General Convention of Texas for four years. During that time, when her field schedule permitted, she was a Beginner superintendent in the First Baptist Church of Dallas. Later she was director of children's work at the First Baptist Church of Muskogee, Oklahoma, and the First Baptist Church of Chattanooga, Tennessee.

Since 1957 Miss Cook has been editor of Beginner lesson courses in the Sunday School Department of the Baptist Sunday School Board. She serves as a Beginner superintendent in the Sunday school and an associate Beginner leader in the Training Union at the First Baptist Church in Nashville.

I Know God Loves Me, a book for four- and five-year-olds, was the author's first book.

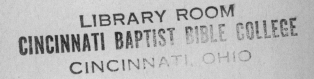

Contents

Church Study Course

THE CHURCH STUDY COURSE began October 1, 1959. It is a merger of three courses previously promoted by the Sunday School Board—the Sunday School Training Course, the Graded Training Union Study Course, and the Church Music Training Course. On October 1, 1961, the Woman's Missionary Union principles and methods studies were added.

The course is fully graded. The system of awards provides a series of five diplomas of twenty books each for Adults or Young People, two diplomas of five books each for Intermediates, and two diplomas of five books each for Juniors. Book awards earned previously in the Sunday School Training Course, the Graded Training Union Study Course, and the Church Music Training Course may be transferred to the new course.

The course is comprehensive, with books grouped into twenty categories. The purpose of the course is to help Christians to grow in knowledge and conviction, to help them to grow toward maturity in Christian character and competence for service, to encourage them to participate worthily as workers in their churches, and to develop leaders for all phases of church life and work.

The Church Study Course is promoted by the Baptist Sunday School Board, 127 Ninth Avenue, North, Nashville, Tennessee, through its Sunday School, Training Union, Church Music, and Church Administration departments; by the Woman's Missionary Union, 600 North Twentieth Street, Birmingham, Alabama; and by the respective departments in the states affiliated with the Southern Baptist Convention. A description of the course and the system of awards may be found in the leaflet "Trained Workmen," which may be obtained without charge from any one of these departments.

A record of all awards earned should be maintained in each church. A person should be designated by the church to keep the files. Forms for such records may be ordered from any Baptist Book Store.

Requirements for Credit in Class
or Home Study

IF CREDIT IS DESIRED for the study of this book in a class or by home study, the following requirements must be met:

I. IN CLASSWORK

1. The class must meet a minimum of seven and one-half clock hours. The required time does not include assembly periods. Ten class periods of forty-five minutes each are recommended. (If laboratory or clinical work is desired in specialized or technical courses, this requirement may be met by six clock hours of classwork and three clock hours of supervised laboratory or clinical work.)

2. A class member who attends all class sessions and completes the reading of the book within a week following the last class session will not be required to do any written work for credit.

3. A class member who is absent from one or more sessions must answer the questions (pp. 149-150) on all chapters he misses. In such a case, he must turn in his paper within a week, and he must certify that he has read the book.

4. The teacher should request an award for himself. A person who teaches a book in the section for Intermediates or Juniors (any category) or conducts an approved unit of instruction for Nursery, Beginner, or Primary children will be granted an award in category 11, Special Studies, which will count as an elective on his own diploma. He should specify in his request the name of the book taught, or the unit conducted for Nursery, Beginner, or Primary children.

5. The teacher should complete the "Request for Book Awards —Class Study" (Form 150) and forward it within two weeks after the completion of the class to the Church Study Course Awards Office, 127 Ninth Avenue, North, Nashville 3, Tennessee.

II. IN HOME STUDY

1. A person who does not attend any class session may receive credit by answering all questions for written work as indicated in the book (pp. 149-150). When a person turns in his paper on home study, he must certify that he has read the book.

2. Students may find profit in studying the text together, but individual papers are required. Carbon copies or duplicates in any form cannot be accepted.

3. Home study work papers may be graded by the pastor or a person designated by him, or they may be sent to the Church Study Course Awards Office for grading. The form entitled "Request for Book Awards—Home Study" (Form 151) must be used in requesting awards. It should be mailed to Church Study Course Awards Office, 127 Ninth Avenue, North, Nashville 3, Tennessee.

III. Credit for This Book

This book is number 1757 in category 17, section for Adults and Young People.

CHAPTER 1

1

A Look at Four- and Five-Year-Olds

JACK BARTON indicated to his pastor and Sunday school superintendent that he would like to become a teacher. He had studied several general teaching books and was conscious of God's leadership in his desire to teach.

Several days later the Beginner superintendent called on Mr. Barton. He seemed to have the qualities she wanted in a worker. Would he like to teach four- and five-year-olds? His insight in regard to teaching was revealed in his first question: "What are four- and five-year-olds like?"

The characteristics and needs of the child determine equipment, curriculum, and teaching methods. His spiritual needs are so inseparably interwoven with his physical, social, mental, and emotional development that we cannot consider one phase without considering all.

I. THE WORLD IN WHICH THEY LIVE

What factors in today's world affect the four- or five-year-old? Is it a good world for him?

1. Some Unwholesome Influences

Today's child is surrounded by many unwholesome influences. Tensions resulting from materialism, concern for financial security, employment of mothers, undesirable TV programs, and general unrest are a part of the life of most young children.

The child lives in a world of hurried adults. Mother is often too tired to give him her best. Although labor-saving devices unheard of in Grandmother's day are found in almost every home, one of the favorite topics of writers in popular magazines is the plight of the average housewife and the tremendous load she carries.

The child lives in a world of preoccupied adults. Shorter work weeks do not necessarily mean that Daddy is at home with the family more. Outside activities often demand much of his time and energy. When he is at home, he may be busy with yard work or a "do it yourself" project, and often cannot give time to the children.

"Keeping up with the Joneses" may have overburdened the family with monthly payments. The trend toward larger families means extra financial burdens. Few people seem to have time to relax and enjoy life. Many mothers are employed outside the home, leaving the children in day care centers or with baby sitters.

The little child's world is too often bounded by the TV screen. The busy mother may use the television set as a free baby sitter, with little supervision given to the programs chosen by the child. The 1959 survey of the National Association for Better Radio and Television reveals that a large majority of the programs for children are objectionable. The child's everyday vocabulary reveals insights into his TV diet. "Murder," "detective," "jail," "robber," "war," "stick-up," "machine gun," and "kill" are words frequently used.

A psychiatrist in a Southern city stated that 80 per cent of his patients were children under twelve years of age. When a Sunday school teacher showed surprise, the doctor's reply was, "The only thing that is surprising to me is that, with all the tensions of today's world, some children escape without having emotional disorders."

2. Some Worthwhile Influences

The picture is not all dark, however. Today's child has advantages denied to children of a generation ago.

Even with its undesirable effects, TV is educational. Some children's programs are excellent. The child's vocabulary and his dramatic play reveal that he knows much more about many more things than his parents did at his age. During a discussion of the creation, one five-year-old enriched the experience for the group by describing in detail one of God's creations unknown to most children of a generation ago—an octopus. He had seen one on TV.

The popularity of child study articles in magazines and of books and periodicals devoted to the study of young children indicates that parents are learning more about the child and his needs. Because of medical advances, the child enjoys better physical fitness than his parents did. He is less frequently absent from Sunday school because of illness than were the children of a past generation.

In the field of religious education, the child today has better opportunities than the child of a generation ago. Increasingly, churches are providing a well-balanced program for preschool children. Families are becoming concerned about the religious training of their children.

In most churches the work in children's departments of the Sunday school is improving. Qualified workers are being enlisted and trained. Studies are being made of the growth needs of children. Emphasis is placed upon the child's learning instead of the teacher's teaching. The child, and not the teacher, is in the limelight. Mature leadership is needed for this new role of the teacher.

II. The Characteristics of Four's and Five's

What kind of child is coming to us out of today's environment? The first thing we observe about four's and five's is that every one is different. God has not made any two of them alike at birth, and no two (even from the same family) have the same environment. There are some characteristics peculiar to all of them, however.

1. *Active*

Perhaps the most obvious characteristic of four- and five-year-olds is that they are active. The child who moves about is not being "bad"; he is being just as God made him to be. Just as the baby in the crib must kick and wave his arms to grow, so the four- or five-year-old must run and jump and skip and hop and crawl and roll. His muscles demand action. The abnormal child is not the one who is active, but the one who is still.

A pedometer revealed that Martia, an unusually quiet five-year-old, walked two and one-half miles in what her mother considered an average day. Wilma June, an active four-year-old, walked five and one-eighth miles in one day. Vickie walked four miles on a day when she spent three hours in kindergarten. (No boy in the study allowed the pedometer to remain on him all day without tampering with it—a revelation of the mechanical curiosity of boys even at four or five.)

What happens when this active child is brought to church and told to be still? He not only does not like it—his entire body rebels. He finds it impossible to be still for more than a few minutes at a time. There are obvious reasons why we cannot give each child the freedom to run and jump and skip and hop and crawl and roll as he wishes, but the program must be planned to provide frequent periods of relaxation from being still.

The question often arises as to whether the child should be allowed to move around in Sunday school instead of learning how to be still so that he will be ready for "church." Usually, the child who has been given opportunities to move about in Sunday school is more likely to be still in the preaching service than the one who has been kept very still in Sunday school. Also a quiet activity time in Sunday school is often followed by an unusually restless group time, and vice versa. Being still (unless he is asleep) is fatiguing for a four- or five-year-old.

2. *Imaginative*

Four- and five-year-olds have vivid imaginations. "Play-like" is a favorite term. A cardboard box may become a hospital, a grocery store, a jet plane, a monkey cage, a submarine, a fire truck, or a jail—all in a period of two hours. Jet planes take off from the back yard while company dinners are served under the shade trees. Four-year-olds often have imaginary playmates.

Imagination is God-given, and is a necessary step to creativeness. Often it is difficult for a child to distinguish between make-believe and truth. Teachers can help him by letting him know that they recognize and appreciate his make-believe.

"There were ten rattlesnakes in my house this morning," imaginative Ken said as he came into the Beginner room.

"My, you make up funny stories!" the teacher replied. "Wouldn't it be bad if there really were rattlesnakes in your house?" Although the teacher recognized Ken's statement as the result of a normal five-year-old's imagination, she made a mental note to watch to see if he were using exaggerations frequently. Habitual use *might* indicate a need to get attention.

3. *Literal-Minded*

Four- and five-year-olds accept literally everything they hear.

"I'm losing my marbles," said a worried mother.

"I'll help you find them," answered Julie, her four-year-old.

"Don't eat the chicken's heart," cried a child. "The preacher said Jesus lives in your heart!"

"What do you think about when you sing 'This Little Light of Mine'?" a father asked his Beginner son.

"Swinging a big flashlight in my hand," was the reply.

In her Sunday school room a child saw a picture of the Good Shepherd. Only after she was grown did she realize that Jesus at no time, so far as we know, ever took care of sheep. Four's and five's are not ready for symbolism. To them, everything is interpreted literally.

4. Creative

According to Webster, "creative" means having the power or quality to produce as a work of thought or imagination. Four's and five's can think through simple problems and work out solutions for themselves if given the opportunity. Give a child building blocks, or crayons, paste, scissors, and paper, or tempera paints and an easel, and observe what he will do with them.

Chuck was drawing a picture with crayons. Carefully he drew a house in the center with trees on each side and a grassy lawn bordered by flowers. Up to this point, he had not been creative; every child in the group had drawn a similar picture. As Chuck sat looking at his picture, he seemed to be troubled. He brought it to the teacher and told her that the grass was too tall and asked her to draw a lawn mower in the yard.

"This is your picture," she told him. "Think about how a lawn mower looks, and then draw it."

In a few minutes Chuck brought his picture to the teacher. He had clipped a picture of a lawn mower from a catalog and had pasted it on his lawn. The idea was entirely his own. Chuck had faced a problem and had solved it creatively.

5. Imitative

Watch how the doll is bathed, diapered, and fed, and you will recognize that children are imitative. A four- or five-year-old boy may even test the temperature of the "milk"

on his arm before giving the bottle to the baby doll. Often the child's expressions will be recognized as those used frequently by his parents. "Where's that knuckle head going?" four-year-old Linda asked, using her daddy's expression.

Let one child start scuffling his feet during group time and soon the entire group will begin it, unless their attention is diverted.

A group of Beginner workers complained to a visiting study course teacher that their children were too loud. They had tried everything but had found no way to get them to work quietly. When the visitor went into their department on Sunday morning, she found that one of the workers had what is generally referred to as a "foghorn voice." The visitor, recognizing that the children were unconsciously imitating the worker, talked with her about her voice. She agreed to whisper for several weeks to help to break herself of the habit of loud talking. Soon nearly every child in the department was whispering.

6. *Curious*

Four's and five's want to know *what* and *why*. How did God make the cocoon change into a moth? What keeps the sun in the sky? How do seed know when it is time to come up? How does the robin learn how to build a nest? Where is God? How did he make the world? The children need grown-up friends who are patient and who will attempt to answer their questions. Sometimes the best answer is, "I don't know, but we'll try to find out." The world has been blessed many times because people were curious and exploring. We should encourage our children to seek knowledge. Attempt to answer each question truthfully and with genuine interest and respect for the child's desire to learn.

7. *Sensitive*

Children are people, and they are sensitive in the same way that adults are sensitive. No little child can have a feeling of friendliness toward the teacher who says, "Everyone come see what a bad thing Jimmy did. Aren't you ashamed, Jimmy?"

Never discuss a child's appearance or behavior in his presence. "Isn't her hair pathetic?" a mother says in the presence of the stringy-haired child. "George can't do anything as well as his sister could at his age," may cause George to be antagonistic toward the person who made the statement as well as toward his sister. It may cause him to withdraw and avoid being with others.

The worker must put herself in the child's place when she finds it necessary to discipline him. If she were being corrected, how would she want it done? She may evaluate her criticism by asking herself, "Would I have been more tactful if I had been dealing with an adult instead of a child?"

8. *Four-Year-Oldness*

Some children are promoted into a Beginner department at the age of three years and six months. Some remain in the age group until the age of six years and almost six months. If there is only one department for four's and five's, the age span it covers can be almost three years.

There is a great deal of difference in the older and younger children in this age group. Although there is no specific time when a child stops being like a three-year-old and starts being like a four-year-old, there are some distinctive traits of each age group. Again, the general characteristics of four's and five's are not the same.

The average four-year-old is dogmatic and bossy. He brags a great deal about what he can do or has done. He likes to talk, and talks a great deal. He frequently talks to himself.

The four-year-old has a sense of humor. Words are funny to him. One group broke into gales of laughter when one child said, "coke, coat, coke, coat." Trying to quiet them would have been like asking adults to refrain from laughing after they had heard a hilarious joke.

Four is sometimes referred to as the age of finding out. Why? and How? are two of the favorite words of four-year-olds. Sometimes they raise these questions merely to make conversation and to get attention; at other times they are genuinely interested in finding the answer. They like to talk about their experiences.

The four-year-old is interested in people. He likes to have other children near, even when he is playing alone. He may cry and hit another child who does not play as he wishes, however, indicating his need for social development.

Since the small muscles are not developed, the four-year-old has difficulty doing such things as cutting on lines, drawing on small paper or with small crayons, or handling small puzzle pieces. He will not be ready for these things until much later.

Four-year-olds have a very short attention span. They will move from one activity to another frequently, and should not be expected to sit still for a long period.

Four-year-olds can accept responsibility for such things as hanging up their coats and putting away materials. Until these activities become fixed habits, however, the child will need frequent reminders.

9. *Five-Year-Oldness*

Five-year-olds are much more ready for group play than they were at four. Frequently groups of three to five children are formed for such activities as block building or dramatic play. When the room is very crowded and there must be more than four or five children in each area, the children will usually form themselves into two groups. Five children may be building a service station on one end of the rug and four more building a church on the other end. They seem to recognize how many can work together well.

Five-year-olds are much more concerned about details than four's. A four-year-old will paint a picture and then decide that it is a truck or a house or a man. A five-year-old may decide what he wants to paint and then fret about how it should be done before he starts painting. He is much more likely to dawdle than a four-year-old.

Five's are better able to distinguish between imaginary and real than four's. Their imagination is still active, but they recognize "playlike" and like to have adults accept their "playlike" stories as such.

They have active minds and like to solve problems. Their attention span has increased. Five's will often work for long periods of time on activities which they initiate themselves. Teacher-initiated activities usually claim their attention for a shorter period of time.

Five's have more emotional control and do not cry as easily as four's. They are more likely to "tell off" another child than to hit him.

Five-year-olds seek approval and affection. They do not

climb into a teacher's lap as often as they did at four, but they thrive on affection and attention.

Physically, the five-year-old's large muscles are still developing, but co-ordination of the small muscles comes at a later time. Like the four-year-old, he is farsighted. He is not ready for writing or small details in coloring, but needs opportunity for wide, sweeping movements (on large sheets of paper) when he paints or draws.

FOR CLASS DISCUSSION

Consider a four- or five-year-old child known by the class members. Does he have the characteristics mentioned in this discussion? Give illustrations of ways in which he has shown these traits.

FOR FURTHER STUDY *

Heron, Frances Dunlap. *Kathy Ann Kindergartner*. New York: Abingdon Press, 1955.

Hymes, James L., Jr. *A Child Development Point of View*. Englewood Cliffs, N. J.: Prentice-Hall, Inc., 1955.

Hymes, James L., Jr. *Understanding Your Child*. Englewood Cliffs, N. J.: Prentice-Hall, Inc., 1952.

Gladys G. Jenkins, Helen Shacter, and William W. Bauer. *These Are Your Children*. Chicago: Albert Whitman and Co., 1953.

Jersild, Arthur T. *Child Psychology*. Englewood Cliffs, N. J.: Prentice-Hall, Inc., 1954. Chaps. 6–10.

Read, Katherine H., *The Nursery School*. Philadelphia: W. B. Saunders Co., 1955.

* In the books listed at the end of each chapter and in those quoted by the author, there may be things which the Baptist Sunday School Board does not endorse. The books are suggested to stimulate discriminatory reading.

CHAPTER 2

I. BASIC NEEDS
    1. Love
    2. Acceptance
    3. Security
    4. Independence
    5. Achievement
    6. Beauty
    7. Guidance and Control
    8. Worship

II. INDIVIDUAL NEEDS
    1. Discovered by Observing and Listening
    2. Discovered by Seeking Information

2

Discovering the Child's Needs

KNOWING the child's characteristics is not enough; we must know his needs. These fall into two areas: those which are basic for all people and those peculiar to the individual.

I. BASIC NEEDS

Physical, mental, social, and spiritual health are dependent upon the meeting of basic needs. Fundamentally, these needs are the same with four-year-olds as they are with sixteen-year-olds or with adults.

1. *Love*

God made people so that they must have love. Physical, mental, emotional, and spiritual growth are dependent upon it. Mental and penal institutions are filled with people suffering from a lack of love.

Four- and five-year-olds must not only have love, they must recognize that they have it. Parents who are not demonstrative, or who are engrossed in the problems of living, sometimes fail to assure the child that they love him. Although they seek to provide the best of everything for him, they do not share their love with him in everyday living. A warm, loving atmosphere in the home, demonstrations of affection, and frequent "I love you's" will reassure the child who doubts his parents' love.

Four-year-old Karen had always been a happy child in Sunday school. She entered into each activity enthusiastically and enjoyed each experience to the fullest. Suddenly the workers noticed a change. She observed much more than she participated. She was not attentive in group time. She whined and began to suck her thumb. One day a worker sat down near her and they began to talk.

"My mother doesn't love me any more," Karen said.

Hiding her surprise at this revelation, the teacher asked, "What makes you think she doesn't?"

"Because she won't let me help her any more. She's always taking care of the baby."

Karen was suffering from a lack of expressed love. She could only interpret her mother's occupation with the new baby as a preference for him over herself. Her suffering was as great as if her mother actually did not love her. Karen probably needed more love from her teachers than any other child in the department.

It is usually the unlovable child who needs love most. The child with dimples and golden curls will be much more likely to receive loving attention than the one with the runny nose and the irritating habits.

A group of nursery school teachers in a professional meeting were asked the question: "What can teachers do about the child who 'rubs them the wrong way'—the child who gets on their nerves? It's hard to respect him, much less to love him." There was a great deal of helpful discussion from the floor. One teacher pointed out that such children usually reminded the teacher of some unhappy experience in her own childhood, some fault of her own which she preferred to ignore, or some other experience for which she felt guilty. Others suggested that they had found that admitting and discussing their feelings with a counselor or with other teachers helped.

Finally a member of the group rose to speak. "My father taught me how to solve that problem," she said. "I just stay on my knees until I love that child."

Love does not mean indulgence. Love that caters to wants

is not real love. The parent or teacher who genuinely loves the child will place the child's *needs* above the child's or the adult's wants or conveniences.

A wrong interpretation of love would tempt us to remove difficulties, to ease their [the children's] way, but they grow and learn through facing life with honesty, clarity and fearlessness.[1]

2. *Acceptance*

Closely related to the need for love is the need for acceptance. The feeling of rejection is one which cuts deeply into each of us. When we feel that we are not accepted by other members of a group, we are frustrated and unhappy.

Carol came from a very poor home. She attended a kindergarten where the other children were from a very different economic background. Each day Carol wore ragged blue jeans; the other children dressed like junior fashion models. Although the teachers tried to help Carol to be accepted by the group, they were not successful. Finally they talked with her mother and suggested that Carol be allowed to wear dresses to school if possible.

There was a difference from the first time Carol appeared in a dress. The other children were not aware that it was old and patched. "Look, Carol has on a dress!" Johnny cried as she entered. For the first time, Carol was accepted by the other children. She participated in all of the group activities and perhaps learned more that day than she had in several previous months of kindergarten.

Children can feel rejected. "Mother won't love you if you do that," or "God only loves good children," do not help a child (who knows he has done some things that are wrong) to feel accepted. "Don't tell me we have another one! Where will we put him?" does not make him feel welcome and accepted at Sunday school.

[1] *The Challenge of Children* (New York: Whiteside, Inc., 1957), p. 47. Used by permission.

"What in the world do you do with him?" a father said in the presence of his four-year-old. "He's without a doubt the worst one I've ever seen." Is it surprising that the child misbehaved, in the light of such rejection by his father?

Each of us—adult and child alike—needs to feel that we are accepted as we are. We are not perfect and our friends know it and we know it, but they accept us as we are. Children need such friends.

3. Security

According to Webster, "security" means freedom from anxiety or doubt. Everyone needs security in order to develop to the best of his ability. Learning may be hindered by a feeling of insecurity.

In what areas may a child have anxiety or doubt?

Perhaps the most common is in respect to his parents' love. Because they fail to assure him over and over that they love him, or because someone has caused him to question their love, a child may have doubts concerning it.

"Daddy won't love you any more. He has a new baby now," an unthinking adult or older child may say to the four- or five-year-old.

Parents may make the child feel insecure by their threats. "Mother and Daddy won't love you if you do that."

The child may feel anxiety or doubt because of unwholesome threats used as punishments. "Don't go behind that counter," a mother was overheard to say to a child as they shopped in a department store. "There's a rat back there that is bigger than you are!"

A child attending one of our assemblies cried all morning. A teacher took him outside to keep him from disturbing the other children. He screamed harder and began to ask, "Where's the policeman?" It was obvious to the teacher that his fears were, in some way, related to a policeman. She shared the experience with the child's father later in the day in an attempt to understand the child's terror. The father laughingly explained that he had told the child that the teacher would call a policeman to get him if he were not good. It is tragic when a child must learn that he cannot believe what his parents tell him.

A child may be insecure because of half-truths he has heard and misinterpreted. Many children have been unable to sleep and have even become physically ill because they have been told the devil would get them. Some have become terrified because of a fear of war or of storms or of floods. One child, who frequently heard his mother criticize his father's driving, became very anxious when the father was out of town on a business trip, fearing that he would be killed in an accident. Frightening stories should not be told in the presence of a child.

The most common insecurity, however, is just a "vague uneasiness" that comes from a feeling of inadequacy. One is never able to relax and be one's best self when this feeling is present. Perhaps an abundance of love is the best treatment. Security comes from having more experiences of being loved and accepted and capable than of being inadequate. Teachers can help the child to have many such positive experiences.

4. Independence

Abundant living and learning require a certain amount of independence. No one can be genuinely happy unless he has the opportunity to make some choices and to do some things for himself. Parents and workers who insist upon "helping" a child make it very difficult for him to be independent. Independence must begin in the early years of life, but the serious problems resulting from a lack of opportunities for independence usually will not be seen until later.

God planned for people to make choices. Even in the

matter of personal salvation, each of us is given the ability to choose. God could have made us perfect creatures, without any choice of our own, but he did not do so.

A visitor in the office of a mental health center remarked to the psychiatrist in charge that it was a pity that a young patient had made an unwise decision in a vitally important matter. The psychiatrist's reply was: "It was the best she could do. Her mother has made every decision for her all her life, and she is rebelling against it. She made that decision because it was the one her mother would not have made. Had the mother not made every choice for her all her life, the daughter would have probably listened to her counsel at this time."

The mother was a devout Christian and thought that she was doing the right thing in keeping her daughter from making unwise decisions. She failed because she was working against the grain of independence which God has placed in every individual.

Where this young woman reacted by rebellion, others may react by passivity. Often such tendencies are not observed in early childhood, but training in independence must begin in the first years of life. Even such small projects as removing his own coat and hanging it up are very important to the child's growth in independence.

Without the ability to think for himself [a person] becomes an easy victim of the advertiser and promoter, willing to believe what is told him in facts, figures and emotion. Because he has not learned to think discriminatingly and independently he cannot weigh the facts and search out the truth, and easily accepts blindly the opinions and convictions of others. His fear of being different forces him to follow mass opinion readily. He cannot be different because he has no independent status, no inner strength with which to be different. He is completely dependent upon the values and decisions of others and must have their flattery and approval for his sustenance.[2]

[2] *Ibid.*, pp. 113–114.

In the area of religion, the dependent person is the one who will "go with the crowd." He will not have the courage to stand up for his convictions—if indeed, he has any convictions of his own. He may drift from one church to another and from one "ism" to another, responding to any appeal which is given to him.

Often teachers can help parents to see the values of giving the child experiences in independence. Teachers themselves must become so sensitive to the child's needs that they can recognize when to give and when to withhold help. This ability grows out of experience and observation, but any teacher who sincerely wishes to do so may acquire the skill.

5. *Achievement*

Every individual needs a feeling of achievement. He must have something which he feels that he does well, or he cannot be his best.

Ray had problems the entire year in the five-year department. He seemed to find new ways of annoying other children and the teachers every Sunday. Seldom did he enter into any constructive activity. At the close of one very trying session, a teacher sat down to try to regain her composure before going to church. Suddenly she tried to put herself in Ray's position. Had anyone ever said anything to him except "Don't"? She doubted it. Had he ever been commended for anything? Probably not. Perhaps a lack of a feeling of achievement was the key to Ray's problem.

Every child should achieve success most of the time. Guide the child who is lacking in self-confidence into activities where he will feel success and importance. Avoid placing him in situations where he will become frustrated by things beyond his ability.

The best way to prepare a child for the hard knocks that life will bring him at five and at fifty is to help him grow in self-confidence by achieving success. We need not plan opportunities for failure; life will bring those. Give him opportunities where success is possible but not easy, and watch him grow.

It is very important, for this reason, that one child not be compared with another. When Johnny has drawn a very crude tree, he may have a feeling of achievement because, to him, it is good. It is better than the one he drew yesterday. If his tree is compared to Mary's, however, his may suffer by comparison. And if the teachers discuss Mary's superior work, or display it on a tackboard, Johnny's suffers even more. Johnny has done his best, but his best has not brought a sense of achievement.

Older five's may be able, with guidance, to recognize that various children in the group have different abilities. Lester is especially good at assuming responsibility at cleanup time and always arranges the blocks neatly; Susan works puzzles faster than anyone; and Jimmy can paint realistic trucks. Unless every child can receive recognition for something he does well, however, this type of discussion may be harmful. Avoid it unless your group is small and unusually mature.

Achievement should bring inner satisfactions rather than outward awards. Although commendation for a job well done is important, the child should not be conditioned to expect praise for each piece of work completed. Undeserved praise will do more harm than good.

Participating in some activity which one does well is often a satisfying outlet for negative feelings. If Johnny is angry, he may forget his anger as he works the very difficult puzzle. The ego-damaging blow which made him angry is forgotten in his sense of achievement.

In the selection of materials, avoid anything which will be too difficult for the children to use with a degree of success. If activities are challenging, but within the ability of the child, growth in self-confidence will take place.

6. *Beauty*

Every child, like every grownup, needs some aesthetic appreciation in order to live his life to the fullest. God has made his world with beauty everywhere, but people must be trained to be aware of it.

Many children have never seen a beautiful flower. They may have stepped on or over the flowers in their own yards without having any appreciation of the beauty of the first spring tulip or the brilliance of the summer marigolds and zinnias. Autumn leaves are enjoyed for their "crunch-crunch" when crushed by little feet on the sidewalk, but the beauty of their coloring has not been experienced by the child.

Some children have not learned to appreciate the beauty of music. The quality of the so-called music they have heard has robbed them of an appreciation of that which is good. Some have never been exposed to good music.

A four-year-old was given the opportunity of listening to portions of Handel's *The Messiah*. No attempt was made to explain the music to her, but her comment was, "It makes me think about Jesus." She asked to hear the records again and again during the following months.

God must love beauty to have conceived of such a beautiful world. Every life will be more abundant when an appreciation of the beauty has been cultivated.

7. *Guidance and Control*

Children must have limits. Someone must say no to them in a firm but friendly way if they are to be secure in their world. They respect the teacher who enforces the necessary restrictions much more than the one who does not.

Four-year-old Sammye threw a temper tantrum because a teacher said no to her demand to be allowed to use equipment in the wrong way. "I hate you! I'm never coming to your Sunday school again! I'll tell my mother on you!" she screamed as she kicked the floor. The teacher ignored her threats and remained firm.

The following Wednesday night the teacher met Sammye's mother in the corridor. "What have you done to charm my Sammye?" she asked. "She has talked all week about how much she loves you!"

Teachers are doing the child an injustice when they give in to him in things that are not for his own good. They should avoid making unnecessary rules, but be consistent in enforcing those which seem necessary. A respect for rules at four and five is the first step toward respect for God's laws and the laws of our country.

8. Worship

God has made man so that he must worship in order to live abundantly. The little child, too, needs a faith in God and experiences in worshiping him. Even a four-year-old can respond to the love of God. "I just love Jesus," Randy said in awe and wonder after he had heard a story.

The person whose other basic needs have been met will be more likely to have satisfying worship experiences. Young children cannot understand all about faith, but they can

easily be led to believe in God and to worship him in love. Jesus expressed his evaluation of the child's ability to respond to God when he used it as an illustration of the response an adult must give (Luke 18:17).

II. Individual Needs

Growing out of the basic needs which are common to everyone, each child has specific needs. Too often workers do not recognize the depth of these individual needs and the importance of understanding them, and they seek only to treat the result rather than the cause.

To ask, "What should I do with a child who is selfish?" is like asking a doctor what should be done for a stomach-ache. The stomach-ache may be a result of eating green apples or of appendicitis or of cancer. Before the doctor can prescribe treatment, he must understand the cause. The selfishness may be the result of too much indulgence or of a lack of attention. Before the teacher can hope to help the child, she must learn why he is unusually selfish.

Behavior problems stem from many causes. Tim's aggressiveness may be altogether different in origin from Bob's, even though they are brothers. There are no "pat answers" for the questions concerning hostility or aggressiveness or shyness or jealousy. The cause of each trait must be discovered and overcome.

Terry cries easily. He becomes very upset if someone accidentally knocks his block tower over. In contrast, Mike will likely laugh, pick up the blocks, and start building again. Before we can help Terry to overcome his insecurity, we must know what has made him insecure.

Ann sits alone most of the time. Usually her finger or thumb is in her mouth. Mary chews the end of her pigtails constantly. What has made them so insecure?

Kent, usually a fairly independent child, suddenly becomes very dependent. He asks for assistance even in taking off his coat. "You do it for me," he says over and over to a teacher. He remains near an adult during the entire session. Kent seems to be seeking assurance that he is loved. Why?

Telling Johnny to stop having temper tantrums or sucking his thumb or becoming frightened when Mother leaves is pointless. We must first find out why Johnny does those things and correct the cause. Just as a doctor may treat one case of skin rash with an ointment and another with a suggestion that the patient refrain from eating strawberries, so the teacher must solve each behavior problem according to its cause. What worked for one child may be very undesirable for another.

1. *Discovered by Observing and Listening*

Betsy stood looking at the fish in the aquarium one Sunday. "I'm bigger than a fish. I'm bigger than a snail. I'm bigger than lots of things," she said quietly to herself. The teacher who overheard her comments realized that Betsy's home problem was more serious than she had suspected. Betsy was told over and over that she was "too little" to do the things that her eight-year-old sister did. Her older sister frequently received special privileges which were denied Betsy because she was "too little."

Detailed notes were made in a department where one child had shown a great deal of hostility. He kicked other children and took their materials away from them. Teachers were beginning to refer to him as being "very naughty."

After several sessions when a recorder made notes on everything he did, a definite behavior pattern emerged. Each time the child had been overly aggressive, the incident followed a question or comment he had made to a teacher. Each time the teacher had ignored him or had answered unsatisfactorily. The recordings gave the teachers the first clue in understanding his behavior, but further study was needed.

A visit in the home will often help in understanding the child's needs, but care must be taken that workers do not jump to conclusions. "Company manners" often cover up the real situation. If the visitor has telephoned to make an appointment for the visit, the child may have been coached so that he does not behave naturally. If the visitor drops in without warning, the mother may be so embarrassed because her hair is in pin curls or the baby is not clean that she does not relax and give a true picture of the home life. Often it takes many visits to establish the friendly relationships with the parents necessary for a thorough understanding of the problems involved.

Many workers find that spending time alone with the child helps in getting to the bottom of his problems and understanding his needs.

Bill had been very aggressive in Sunday school, and no one had been able to make friends with him. He disliked all the other children and refused to work with any of them. They, in turn, disliked him. The teachers felt that his problems were very serious.

It was difficult to visit in Bill's home because the parents were both shift workers in a factory. The mother worked during the day and the father at night. When they were at home, one or the other was usually asleep. An appointment was made for a visit with the mother, who was not a Christian. The worker did not feel free to discuss Bill's problems with her. She did not seem to be a mature person and would likely have taken Bill out of Sunday school, feeling that the teachers could not handle him. They talked casually about Bill, and the teacher tactfully led the mother to talk about the home relationships.

The picture of the home life was not a pretty one. Bill went to kindergarten in the morning but played alone at home in the afternoon until an older brother came home from school. The father was at home during that time, but was sleeping. The mother admitted that the father became very angry when Bill waked him. The mother came home late in the afternoon, exhausted from a day at the factory. Bill wanted much more of her time and energy than she was willing to give him.

Later the same teacher who had talked with the mother visited Bill. Arrangements had been made for her to pick him up at home and take him to the drugstore for a soda.

The teacher did not pry into Bill's home background, but remained quiet most of the afternoon. Although Bill had seldom talked to the teachers in Sunday school, he talked very freely during the hour or more that he spent with the teacher. He told her that his daddy really was mean when he was drunk. He said the neighbors wouldn't let him (Bill) play with their children because they said he was bad, but he didn't care; he didn't like them anyway. It was obvious to the teacher that he wanted to play with the neighbor children very much, and that the rejection he received from them was a part of his problem.

Bill said that he didn't like his mother or his daddy or his brother because they were all mean to him. He assured the teacher that no one loved him but his grandmother, and he wanted to run away and live with her.

The teacher could understand Bill's hostility after learning these things about his background. She recognized that not all of Bill's story could be accepted as truth—but it was his family life as he saw it, and that was the important thing. Perhaps his daddy really did get drunk and beat him, or perhaps that was an expression he had heard and did not even understand. In either event, it showed that he did not have a good relationship with his father. Whether or not his parents loved him was not as important as whether Bill thought they loved him.

What Bill needed most was a friend, and he found one in the teacher. Although she could not make up for the tragic

SUNDAY SCHOOL INFORMATION SHEET

Child's name _____

What do you usually call him? _____

Date of his birth _____

Father's name _____ Occupation _____

Father Christian? _____ Member of what church? _____

In Sunday school? _____ Mother Christian? _____ Member of what church? _____ In Sunday school? _____ Are parents divorced? _____ Separated? _____ Is the mother employed outside the home? _____ Where? _____

Works from _____ until _____ (time)

Child stays with _____ while mother works.

Does entire family read the Bible and pray together each day? _____

Do you offer thanks at meals? _____ Does the child say a bedtime prayer _____ Memorized prayer or his own words? _____

Other children in family (give names and ages) _____

_____

Who are his closest friends? What are their ages? _____

_____

What does your child like to play? _____

What pets does he have? _____

What TV programs does he watch regularly? _____

As far as you know, has anything happened at church to give him any unhappy experience? If so, what? _____

_____

How often does someone read to him? _____

Does he enjoy books and stories? _____ What are his favorites? _____

Does he attend morning worship? _____ Sunday evening service? _____ Wednesday night? _____

What home duties does he have (such as putting away toys or setting the table)? _____

Does he attend kindergarten? _____ Nursery school? _____

Does he have any of the following fears:

Of animals? _____   Of storms? _____

Of darkness? _____   Of unusual sounds? _____

Of people? _____   Of God or the devil? _____

Is he shy? _____ Does he lack confidence? _____ Is he nervous? _____ Does he have a feeling of inferiority? _____

Is he stubborn? _____ Is he selfish? _____ Is he jealous? _____

Does he demand attention? _____

Please list any special needs which you would like for us to consider this year, and anything about your child that will be of help to us in understanding him.

home background, she did give him her love and affection, and it made a difference in Bill's attitude.

The information concerning Bill's family was kept in strictest confidence. Other workers in the department were told part of the story, but all agreed that it should not be repeated outside the group.

2. *Discovered by Seeking Information*

Sometimes the needs cannot be discovered by observation and listening, but additional information may be secured by asking. Many workers use an information sheet (see p. 27) to help them to get a better picture of the background of each child. Such a questionnaire will never take the place of visits and personal contacts, but often the additional information is helpful.

The questionnaire may be taken into the home by the worker and explained to the parents. An appointment may be made for the worker to call again to pick it up, or the parent may be asked to bring it to Sunday school the following Sunday. In some instances, an addressed, stamped envelope may be left with the questionnaire so that it can be mailed when it is completed.

FOR CLASS DISCUSSION

Ben is already six and is the largest child in his department. He has an older brother and sister, and his parents are very faithful, loyal church workers.

Ben seems to be a very unhappy child. He constantly does things which he knows will annoy his teachers. For instance, he often slips up to the easel and paints the outside of the jars.

In his presence, his father told the teachers that Ben was one of the worst children he had ever seen and that they should punish him in any way they wished.

Ben has seemed to enjoy two things in the department. One

Sunday the group had been finger painting, and the teacher asked Ben (who had not participated but had disturbed the others) to wash the bowl she had used to mix the paints. She explained to him that it would break, but that she would trust him to care for it.

On another occasion a doctor kit was used. Ben and another child almost fought over it. On the Sundays that Ben was the doctor, he thoroughly enjoyed working with the other children. He did not show any undesirable aggressive tactics. When he did not get to be the doctor, however, he caused trouble constantly.

He seems to be above average in intelligence but is very unpopular with the other children.

If you were Ben's teacher, what additional information would you like to have about him? How would you try to get this information? From the information which you have, what would you say is the greatest need? (Additional information might throw new light on this subject.) In what ways would you try to meet this need if Ben were in your department?

FOR FURTHER STUDY

Baruch, Dorothy. *New Ways in Discipline*. New York: Whittlesey House, 1949.

Heffernan, Helen. *Guiding the Young Child*. Boston: D. C. Heath and Co., 1959. Appendix 1.

Heinz, Mamie W. *Growing and Learning in the Kindergarten*. Richmond: John Knox Press, 1959. Chap. 2.

Jenkins, Shacter, and Bauer. *These Are Your Children*. Chicago: Albert Whitman and Co., 1953.

Read, Katherine H. *The Nursery School*. Chaps. 7–12.

The Challenge of Children. (Compilation). New York: Whiteside, Inc., 1957. Chaps. 2, 5, 11, 12, 13, 14.

Saul, Leon J., M. D. *Emotional Maturity*. Philadelphia: J. B. Lippincott Co., 1947.

Willis and Stegeman. *Living in the Kindergarten*. Chicago: Follett Publishing Co., 1953. Part I.

CHAPTER 3

I. MEANING OF TEACHING

II. OBJECTIVES OF TEACHING

III. ELEMENTS IN THE TEACHING-LEARNING SITUATION

IV. TEACHING FOR EVANGELISM
1. Recognition of Existence of God
2. Recognition That Jesus Is God's Son
3. Recognition of God's Love
4. Recognition of Personal Sin and of God's Righteousness
5. Recognition of God's Plan of Salvation
6. Ability to Make Decisions

3

Teaching to Bring About Changes

WE DO NOT KNOW just how a child learns. God's plan for growth is miraculous, and the child grows and changes before our eyes. He learns to walk and talk, to use his arms, his hands, and then his fingers. One day we discover that he is thinking for himself. He has reasoned through a problem and has found an answer. Perhaps it is not the best answer, but it is his. His growth is so rapid that we are challenged and frightened by our responsibility in guiding him.

I. MEANING OF TEACHING

The retention of facts is not learning in its fullest sense. Only as these facts can be applied in the child's life are they meaningful. Even Bible verses and stories must be related to his daily living and level of understanding. The rich young ruler who came to Jesus (Matt. 19:16–22) knew the Scriptures and knew what he should do to inherit eternal life, but this knowledge did not save him. For a little child to be able to repeat many Bible verses and stories is good—but only if he applies them to his everyday life. Memorizing "Be ye kind" does not automatically make a child kind, or even make him want to be kind.

Learning takes place only when a change has been brought about in the pupil. Teaching the Bible is more than a sharing of Bible facts. It involves change in attitudes, habits, ideas, and ideals.

A four-year-old was overheard saying to a playmate, "If you don't be kind to me like the Bible says, I'll beat you over

31

the head with this shovel." Had he learned "Be ye kind"? He could *repeat* it, but he could not *live* it. Spiritual truths must be used in everyday living before learning is completed.

II. OBJECTIVES OF TEACHING

Since teaching is changing, the teacher must understand the areas in which changes are needed. The following are over-all objectives as prepared by the Education Division of the Baptist Sunday School Board.

A. *Christian Conversion*

Our aim is to lay early foundations through the child's continuing experiences which will lead him toward the time when he is capable of accepting Jesus as his personal Saviour. This means helping each child:

1. to feel that God loves him at all times;
2. to realize that there are some things that please God and to love God and to want to please him;
3. to learn that the Bible is a special book that helps us know how to please God;
4. to think of Jesus as his friend and helper.

B. *Church Membership*

Our aim is to begin to lay foundations for an understanding of what it means to be a member of a church. This means helping each child:

1. to think of his church as a place where he has happy experiences;
2. to grow in his ability to participate in church worship services with his family;
3. to feel that he is a part of the church life.

C. *Christian Worship*

Our aim is to help each child to have moments of satisfying worship experiences and to grow in his ability to participate in group worship. This means helping each child:

1. to know that he can talk to God at any time and anywhere;
2. to have satisfying experiences in talking to God;
3. to grow in his ability to participate in group worship with children of his own age;

4. to develop a growing appreciation for beautiful surroundings, music, Bible passages that are read aloud, prayer, the offering, and the preacher's message.

D. *Christian Knowledge and Conviction*

Our aim is to help each child to know that the Bible is a special book which tells about God and Jesus and that the people of his church help others to know about God and Jesus. This means helping each child:

1. With respect to the Bible—
   (1) to begin to understand that God helped men know what to write in the Bible;
   (2) to become familiar with some of the surroundings and customs of the people the Bible tells about;
   (3) to enjoy hearing Bible stories and verses;
   (4) to grow in his understanding of Bible truths and learn to relate them to his own experiences;
   (5) to grow in his realization that the Bible is God's way of telling us how to live happily with others;
   (6) to know that the Bible was meant for all people.

2. With respect to the great realities of the Christian faith—
   (1) to know that God made the world and everything in it;
   (2) to know that Jesus can do things that no one else can do, because he is God's Son.

3. and 4. With respect to his church, denomination, and the larger Christian movement—
   (1) to know that there have been churches for a long, long time;
   (2) to know that his church is one of many churches all over the world;
   (3) to know ways his church and other churches help people to know about Jesus;
   (4) to know that the money brought to church is used to help others know about Jesus.

E. *Christian Attitudes and Appreciations*

Our aim is to guide each child in the development of attitudes and appreciations that will encourage personal growth. This means helping each child:

1. and 2. Regarding God and the meaning of existence—
   (1) to experience a deepening reverence for God's power

and greatness; to accept the fact that God made the world; and to have a growing appreciation of ways God cares for the things in it;

(2) to love God and to want to do the things that please him;

(3) to trust God as the one who loves and cares for all people; to feel that God is near and that one can talk to God any time, anywhere; to want to talk to God;

(4) to feel thankful for the many ways God helps him;

(5) to grow in awareness of the difference between fantasy and reality.

3. Regarding self—

(1) to feel secure in God's world, because he is an important part of God's plan;

(2) to begin to realize that God made him and gave him the ability to think, to make choices and decisions, and to be creative; to begin to realize that people are more important than any other thing God made;

(3) to realize that God wants him to have a strong, healthy body and to use it in ways pleasing to God;

(4) to realize that God can help him in ways that no one else can;

(5) to want to do things in ways pleasing to Jesus and to want to grow in the ways in which Jesus grew.

4. Regarding others—

(1) to realize that it is a part of God's plan for people to be friendly and to help one another;

(2) to grow in his appreciation of others and what they do for him;

(3) to develop in his ability to share, to work, and to play happily with others;

(4) to accept the fact that God made and loves all people and to have kind attitudes toward them;

(5) to want others to know about Jesus.

5. Regarding the Bible and divine institutions—

(1) to develop a growing love for the Bible and a growing appreciation for ways it can help him in everyday life;

(2) to grow in his understanding of the importance of his church;

    (3) to think of Sunday as a special day of worship and activities pleasing to God;

    (4) to think of happy homes as a part of God's plan;

    (5) to grow in his appreciation of people in authority and in his willingness to co-operate with them.

6. Regarding the present world—

    (1) to feel that the world God made is good and that nature, work, and the ability to do many things are gifts of God;

    (2) to want to help others in making his (the child's) world a better place.

F. *Christian Living*

Our aim is to help each child to develop habits and to have experiences which encourage his spiritual growth. This means helping each child:

1. to begin to accept the Bible as a guide for his conduct in everyday life;

2. to grow in his understanding of prayer and in his ability to pray;

3. to want to do things in ways pleasing to Jesus;

4. to grow in his ability to make right choices;

5. to develop in his ability to help make his home happy;

6. to have an increasing love for all people which he will express in friendliness and co-operation.

G. *Christian Service*

Our aim is to help each child to grow in his desire and ability to help others. This means helping each child:

1. to tell others about Jesus;

2. to be a helper in his home and church;

3. to be happy as he gives his money to help others know about Jesus;

4. to do helpful things for others;

5. to begin to accept his limited abilities and to help as best he can;

6. to receive satisfaction from doing things with others;

7. to participate in group activities that make others happy.[1]

[1] Based on *The Curriculum Guide,* (Nashville: Convention Press, 1960).

The teacher's task is to bring about changes in the child's attitudes, behavior, and knowledge. Each of the three is important. Behavior is often determined by attitudes, and attitudes are often affected by knowledge.

III. ELEMENTS IN THE TEACHING-LEARNING SITUATION

We have seen that learning to repeat a Bible verse, such as "Be ye kind," is not the primary lesson to be learned in Sunday school. Until the child has learned to apply the verse to his life, the desired learning has not been completed. How does a child learn "Be ye kind"?

First of all, the child must understand what being kind means. The only way he can gain this understanding is through experience. Verbalizing is inadequate. Suppose the child is building with blocks. He is having a good time until he needs a certain block which another child is using. The other child shares it with him willingly. The teacher may remark, "That was a kind thing for you to do. You remind me of the Bible verse, 'Be ye kind.'"

The child has learned that sharing blocks is kind. He has had a concrete experience with the concept "kindness" and has felt satisfaction in the result because of the teacher's approval. Another time he may learn that helping a friend button his smock is kind, and on another that showing a new friend where to hang up his coat is kind. Gradually he begins to form a concept of the meaning of kindness that will prepare him to face a situation he has never faced before and recognize the kind thing to do.

Not only must he understand the meaning of kindness; he must have some reason for being kind (motivation). To the mature Christian, the fact that the Bible says for him to be kind is an adequate motive. This is not true for the young child until he has a love and appreciation for the Bible. The child must receive a feeling of satisfaction from being kind. If his parents and teachers have expressed approval of his kindness, satisfaction will result. He will have a good feeling because he has done the "right" thing. The feeling of satisfaction based on human approval is not the highest motive, but it is the one the child will experience first.

Then he must be able to see that kindness "works." Everyone has a better time using the various Sunday school materials when he is kind.

How can we lead the child to be kind because he loves Jesus and because Jesus is pleased when he is kind?

First, we must show the child our love for Jesus and our desire to do the things which please him. "Much talking" is not the answer, but rather quiet, day-by-day living before the child and the application of Christ's teachings to our lives in ways the child can recognize. The Spirit-filled teacher will have no difficulty in this area. In the way that she talks about Jesus and uses the Bible she will reveal that Jesus and the Bible are special to her.

By helping the child to grow in his knowledge of Jesus as a kind and loving person, we help him to learn to love Jesus. Knowing the stories of Jesus' kindness to the lepers, the children, and Zacchaeus helps the child to grow in his concept of Jesus. By helping him to think of Jesus as his personal friend, we help him to grow toward the desired goals. Such goals cannot be reached in one Sunday. Most of us do not completely learn "Be ye kind" in a lifetime.

These same principles apply in the teaching of all Bible truths. Through his activities the child gains an understanding of the meaning of the Bible truth and its application to his problems. His objective is seldom the same as the teacher's, because she must reach him through his interest. He does not build with blocks to learn a Bible truth; he is doing it because he is interested in block building.

The materials with which he is working, the guidance given by the teacher, and the other children involved, provide the *stimulus* for learning. Motivation comes from the experience and from the concepts he is learning. His *response* (which may be mental, emotional, or physical) is essential to the learning situation. He may respond to one situation by giving the block to Billy when Billy asks for it, indicating that he has learned. He may respond to another situation emotionally or mentally. The *satisfaction* he receives will determine whether he will repeat this reaction in similar situations in the future.

IV. TEACHING FOR EVANGELISM

By far the greatest change that can come to any person is the change that comes when he accepts Jesus as his personal Saviour. Rarely does this experience come before Primary or Junior years, and teachers do not present all the claims of the gospel to four- and five-year-olds. However, there are some things that are essential before a person is ready for a full response to the gospel, and teachers of four- and five-year-olds help to lay the foundation. The experiences of the four- and five-year-old, plus the additional steps made during later years, will prepare him for the work of the Holy Spirit which must come *in God's own time.*

1. *Recognition of Existence of God*

Before a person is ready to become a Christian, he must believe that there is a God. It is not difficult for a child to believe in something he has not seen, but his problem is to differentiate between fanciful and real. Santa Claus and Superman are often confused with God.

(1) As teachers we try to make God real by pointing out things he has done. Nature materials are used extensively. The child sees the bird's nest and learns that God helps birds know how to make it; he learns that God made the tadpole change into a frog, and made the flowers grow from the seed.

(2) We try to make God real by relating him to the child's everyday experiences. "I'm glad for your new sweater. God

planned for sheep to grow wool. He helps people know how to make sweaters from the wool."

(3) We try to make God real by learning to talk to him. We talk to God in the child's language about the things in his everyday experiences.

(4) We try to make God real by the use of Bible stories that tell about him. Perhaps the creation story and the story of God sending his Son are the most effective.

2. *Recognition That Jesus Is God's Son*

Before a person is ready to become a Christian, he must believe that Jesus is God's Son.

(1) With four- and five-year-olds this belief is built up largely through stories and informal conversation. When children hear of Jesus' birth, they learn that Jesus was God's Son and that "God . . . loved us, and sent his Son."

(2) Children learn that Jesus can do many things that other people cannot do, because he is God's Son.

3. *Recognition of God's Love*

Before a person becomes a Christian, he must accept the fact that God and Jesus love him.

The child learns to say "I love you" early in life because it is a magic phrase that earns adult acceptance and approval. We can help him to learn the meaning of love, not by telling him what it is, but by showing him what it is. Not only must the teacher love the child; he must believe that she loves him. She must demonstrate this love over and over by acceptance, approval, and, when necessary, restraint.

During the time that we are trying to help the child learn the meaning of love, we are telling him that Jesus and God love him. We help him to appreciate the things that God planned for him as evidences of his love. We want him to know that God sent Jesus to tell us of his love. Some four-year-olds are ready for this concept.

4. *Recognition of Personal Sin and of God's Righteousness*

Before a person becomes a Christian, he must know that he is a sinner, that God is righteous, and that only through Christ can one become righteous. The four- or five-year-old can learn that some things are right and some are wrong. His gauge for determining right and wrong is usually whether he gains approval or disapproval for it.

5. *Recognition of God's Plan of Salvation*

Before a person becomes a Christian, he must believe that Jesus' death is the only way of salvation. Four- and five-year-olds, on the whole, are not emotionally and mentally mature to the extent that they can be taught the truths of eternal judgment, the atonement, or even the crucifixion and resurrection. However, teachers can lay the foundations for these concepts.

(1) We can help the child understand that we love him even when he is "bad." This is the first step in learning that God loves him even when he sins. This truth is often presented through the story of Zacchaeus.

(2) We can help the child begin to understand forgiveness by demonstrating it. Without using the word "forgive," we will practice it by forgiving the child when he does wrong. Later he will learn the word "forgive."

6. *Ability to Make Decisions*

Before a person can become a Christian, he must be able to make a decision. Very few four's and five's are ready for this decision. However, developing ability to choose helps to prepare the child for the time when he will face life's greatest decision—the matter of salvation.

We give the four- or five-year-olds many activities which help them to develop in self-confidence. Creative activities in which the emphasis is on the process rather than on the product, discipline which does not destroy self-confidence, and loving acceptance—all will contribute toward such development.

Each child will have opportunities to make many choices each Sunday. He will choose the activity in which he will participate, and, to a large measure, choose how he will use the materials made available.

This entire field of teaching and learning is one which all of us who teach four's and five's should study further. Learning is one of God's miracles. We cannot keep a normal child from learning, but we can give him experiences to make his learning more worthwhile.

FOR CLASS DISCUSSION

Study the Bible stories in a current issue of *Beginner Teacher*. To which objective is each story most closely related?

FOR FURTHER STUDY

Campbell, Doak S. *When Do Teachers Teach*. Nashville: Convention Press, 1935.

Edge, Findley B. *Teaching for Results*. Nashville: Broadman Press, 1956.

Price, J. M. *Jesus the Teacher*. Nashville: Convention Press, 1946.

Smart, James. *The Teaching Ministry of the Church*. Philadelphia: The Westminster Press, 1954.

Washburn, Ruth Wendell. *Children Know Their Friends*. New York: William Morrow and Co., Inc., 1949.

CHAPTER 4

4

Teaching Through Activities

Jesus set the example for us in teaching methods. Even with adults he used activity teaching. To give meaning to the words, "I will make you fishers of men" he guided a fishing activity. To make clear the truth, "I am the bread of life" he enlisted the disciples in the work of feeding the five thousand. The activity procedure Jesus used with adults is even more necessary with little children.

I. THE PLAN OF ACTIVITY TEACHING

We follow Jesus' example by using the everyday experiences in the child's world to teach him spiritual truths. If we help him to feel that Jesus loves him, we have not failed.

The child's life cannot be divided into segments; his social, emotional, mental, and physical growth cannot be separated from his spiritual growth. In Sunday school the child is given opportunities to work with such materials as paints, blocks, dolls, dishes, play dough, books, puzzles, nature materials, and clay. These materials are selected because the experiences which the child has with them can be effectively related to the objectives stated in chapter 2. Spiritual teaching, to be effective, must be an inseparable part of the activities of the child as he uses the tangible materials.

The use of songs, Bible verses, religious conversation, prayer, and worship, is interwoven into the use of the tangible materials. It is this interwoven spiritual teaching which lifts the activities with four's and five's above the level of the secular kindergarten program.

Group time follows activity time and builds upon the experiences which the children have had in the more informal period. *Activity time is, to a certain extent, a testing time for the teaching which is done in group time*. Teachers can observe the children in informal situations and determine many of their growth needs.

The length of the three parts of the Sunday morning session (activity time, cleanup time, and group time) will be determined by the age of the children. Activity time should begin when the first child arrives and be followed by cleanup time. In the Sundays immediately after Promotion Day, group time for four-year-olds should last about fifteen minutes. For more mature children the period will be longer. When four- and five-year-olds are in the same department, the length of activity time should be planned to meet the needs of the average child.

Workers should arrive early enough to have all materials ready and be on hand to greet the early arrival. Problems arise when the child has to "wait until Sunday school begins."

Workers should provide as many activities as feasible, considering the space, equipment, and number of children. There should usually be not less than one activity for every five children, and more if possible. Each child as he comes may choose from the various activities provided. When he has finished what he has started, he may move on to another activity if he desires.

During activity time one of three plans may be followed: (1) Each teacher may be assigned to a specific activity, such as books, blocks, or nature materials; (2) each teacher may be assigned to a general area of the room; or (3) no assignments may be given, leaving the workers free to help wherever they are needed. There are advantages and disadvantages in each plan, and each department should determine which one best meets its needs.

When there is a teacher assigned to each activity, she

may have a tendency to dominate the group and talk too much, or else feel that she is wasting her time by not *doing* something all the time. If she remains too close to the group, she will keep the children from being as free as they would otherwise be. When no assignments are made, workers may get together in one area of the room and neglect the needs of the children. Careful planning can avoid either extreme.

Before group time the superintendent will alert each group to begin putting away materials. Since some require more time than others, a reminder to each group at whatever time the superintendent feels is necessary is better than a general signal. Often a reminder from a teacher may be wise: "It will soon be cleanup time, so perhaps you'd better not start another puzzle." Children should be responsible for putting away materials they have used, with the assistance and encouragement of the teachers.

Our plans for activity time are based on these beliefs about four- and five-year-olds:

1. Children like to do things for themselves, and they learn through doing things for themselves.
2. Children have a more sustained interest in activities which they initiate themselves.
3. Children, like adults, do not like to work with someone looking over their shoulders all the time.
4. Children need controls; someone must say no in a firm, but friendly way.
5. Children need routine guidance in working together and in the use of materials.

The most common activities used are homeliving, nature, blocks, books, art materials, puzzles, and records. Other special activities will be added from time to time.

II. Teaching Through Homeliving Materials

Children have many happy learning experiences as they use homeliving materials.

A ROOM ARRANGEMENT FOR ACTIVITY TEACHING

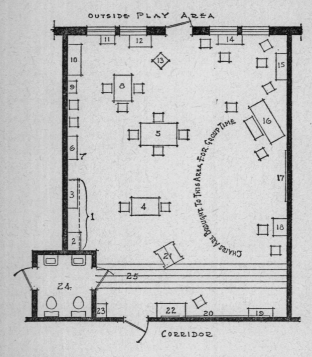

1. Overhead Storage Cabinet
2. Table for Reports
3. Rack for Children's Wraps
4. Table for Puzzles
5. Table for Art Activities
6. Art Shelves
7. Puzzle Rack on Shelf
8. Table for the "Home"
9. Stove
10. Cabinet-Sink
11. Chest of Drawers
12. Doll Bed
13. Rocking Chair
14. Nature Shelves
15. Bookrack
16. Piano
17. Picture Rail
18. Table-Cabinet and Record Player
19. Block Shelves
20. Tackboard
21. Painting Easel
22. Drying Rack
23. Rack for Adult Wraps
24. Bathroom (connecting another room)
25. Floor Staff

ROOM SIZE—24'-0" x 32'-0"

This room is designed to accommodate 25 children and 5 workers. It will accommodate 20 children for weekday kindergarten.

1. *Materials Which May Be Used*

Materials which are chosen should be those which encourage creative play centered around the idea of everyday living in the home. Equipment should be child size rather than doll size, and should be sturdy enough to be used in the way that adults use similar equipment in the home.

If there is adequate space, the home may include a table, cabinet-sink, stove, doll bed, rocking chair, chest of drawers, doll, and dishes. Substitutions can be made when not all of these are available or when space is limited. Orange crate and apple box furniture is used in many churches with limited budgets.

Dishes should be of polyethylene plastic—a soft plastic which will not break. Usually such dishes cannot be found in the toy departments, but adult-size salad plates and juice glasses are the ideal size. Many workers prefer not to use cups, since they want to encourage the children to drink milk or fruit juice instead of coffee or tea. A small pitcher may be provided for the playlike milk. These polyethylene dishes may be purchased from special dealers if they are not available in department stores.

Cooking utensils may be of good quality aluminum or aluminum-copper combination, if the church has adequate funds. Many departments find the foil plates used for individual-size frozen pies and small frozen casseroles satisfactory when nothing else is available. Small saucepans bought in the housewares section of a store are usually more durable, and more nearly the correct size, than those found in toy departments.

From time to time, dress-up clothes may be provided for homeliving play. Women's hats, purses, blouses and skirts, and occasionally, costume jewelry, may be used for the girls. Boys will enjoy men's hats, ties, and coats.

Doll clothes should be provided, since children enjoy dressing and undressing the dolls. Many workers feel that baby dolls are more worthwhile than teen-age or "little girl" dolls. Clothes should open down the back and fasten with snaps instead of buttons, for easy removal by little fingers. Blankets, bottles, diaper bags, and other baby accessories suggest many activities to the children.

Doll clothes and bed linens should be clean at all times. If there is no room for a chest of drawers, clothes may be kept in a small suitcase or shoe box.

Play dough is used extensively. Such brands as "Play-Doh" are available from your Baptist Book Store. Some workers use wall paper cleaner. An inexpensive dough may be made from two parts of flour and one part salt, with enough water to make it the right consistency for kneading. Color with food coloring if desired. Add a small amount of salad oil to keep the dough moist.

Keep play dough tightly sealed when it is not in use. An airtight polyethylene container is best, but plastic bags, closed with rubber bands, may be used. For use with the dough, provide small rolling pins (pieces of broom handle may be used), cooky cutters, and pans for baking.

From time to time, add milk cartons (thoroughly rinsed), small vegetable or fruit cans, or pictures of wholesome prepared foods, mounted on cardboard. If tin cans are used, remove the bottom rather than the top of the can, and be sure there are no sharp edges.

2. Suggested Activities and Guidance

Children have vivid imaginations and will initiate their own activities if challenging materials are provided. Workers will usually not find it necessary to suggest experiences. Provide the materials, keep in the background, and you will see such activities as the following (or others just as worthwhile) take place: cooking and eating meals; shopping for groceries; caring for the baby; going to church; going on trips; cleaning house; getting the playlike children ready for school; entertaining company; gathering vegetables from the garden.

The activities the children initiate will be determined by the experiences they have had in their own homes during the previous week, or by other events which have made a deep impression on their minds.

Should the teacher participate in the play? Usually not, unless there is a special invitation for her to do so. Frequently she may be invited to be the guest for dinner or to play the part of a grandmother or visiting friend. She should join in naturally on such occasions, taking care that she does not dominate the play.

Cooking the eggs in the oven may not seem logical to her, but if the children are satisfied, she will do well to let them use their own ideas. She is more concerned about their learning how to work together than about their learning how to cook eggs.

3. *Values of These Experiences*

One of the most valuable benefits of the homeliving experiences is the opportunity they provide for testing teaching. The alert teacher can learn such things as the following by carefully observing (if the children are not conscious of her observation): Have the children learned to share? Are they kind? Do they accept responsibility? Do they thank God for food, read the Bible, or use religious conversation naturally in the home? Have any teachings been misinterpreted? In what areas does teaching need to be strengthened?

The "mother" in the home asked the "sister" to bring the baby's milk. "We don't have any, but I'll go to the store," the sister volunteered.

When the purchase had been made and the baby's bottle prepared, the child who was the playlike mother bowed her head. "Thank you, God, for the baby's milk," she said.

"You don't have to thank God for it," the sister remarked. "I was the one who went to the store for it, not God."

The teacher who was observing unobtrusively, learned an area where positive teaching was needed. Wisely she did not interrupt the fascinating make-believe to "preach" at that moment. Rather, she made a mental note to be alert for the time when the children would be ready for a guided conversation on how God provides. At the next teachers' meeting she shared the incident with the other workers, and they all discussed ways of meeting this need.

Homeliving experiences give meaning to the spiritual truths being taught. It is easy for a child to hear and even repeat, "We . . . are helpers" (2 Cor. 1:24); "Be ye kind" (Eph. 4:32); "Be gentle unto all" (2 Tim. 2:24) and many other Bible verses or truths, without relating them to actual life experiences. Homeliving activities are very similar to those which the child experiences at home, and verses learned in this setting are likely to be recalled and used in similar situations at home.

Just as an adult is not helped by memorizing the plan of salvation if he does not accept Jesus, so the child is not benefited by Bible teaching if he does not relate it to life. As he takes his turn in using the rolling pin or rocking the baby, as he discovers that playing is no fun when Jimmy snatches all the dough, or as he receives a feeling of satisfaction and achievement from arranging the dishes neatly on the shelf, Bible teaching is beginning to live for him. He is learning that the Bible tells him how to work and play happily with others. Each year of his spiritual development he will receive further insights into the application of Bible teachings to his own life.

Homeliving experiences reveal much about the child's own home. The playlike mother will usually treat her children as her own mother treats her, or as she wishes her mother would treat her, or as she expects her mother to treat her.

Many children are not secure and happy in strange surroundings. To them homeliving experiences are very valuable. Because they can play out doing the things they see Mother and Daddy doing every day, they feel more secure in the department. They often play alone, although other children are in the area at the same time. For example, four-year-olds will frequently work individually in making cookies or pies or string beans from dough, ignoring others who may be preparing another meal at the same table or cabinet.

The homeliving activities relate directly to many of the objectives outlined in chapter 3. For example, they help the child to think of church as a happy place, to practice worship experiences, to feel secure, to make choices and decisions, to be creative, to realize that helping one another is part of God's plan, to share, to work together, to think of home as part of God's plan, to grow in appreciation of people in authority. Home is the little child's world. The homeliving play provides a link between the shy child and the experiences in his Sunday school room.

III. Teaching Through Nature Materials

Jesus used nature extensively in his teachings. He referred to the lilies of the field, the sower and the seed, the sparrows, the foxes and their holes, the vineyard, and many other objects from the everyday world.

1. *Materials Which May Be Used*

An open shelf, placed near a window if possible, is needed for nature materials. These materials should be changed at least once a month or they will become meaningless for the children. There is value in having at least one new object each Sunday.

Every community has many nature objects which are fascinating to little children. The alert teacher can find new ones every day. They may fall into the following areas:

Living things (fish, turtles, parakeets, tadpoles, horned toads, lizards, grasshoppers, moths, butterflies, earthworms, ants, snails, chipmunks, baby rabbits or squirrels, hamsters, guinea pigs, and many others)

Homes of animals (birds' nests, shells, hornets' nests, dried mud from the top of crayfish holes, cocoons)

Growing things (fresh flowers, potted plants, various kinds of seeds and seed pods, buds from springtime plants, autumn leaves)

Products God provides (wheat, flour, and bread; ear corn, meal, and corn bread or corn flakes; cotton boll, cotton thread, and cotton cloth; wool, yarn, and woolen cloth; sand and bricks; bark and lumber)

Along with these materials, add to the nature shelf books or pictures which give interesting information about the materials displayed.

Nature materials should be found all over the room, not just on the nature shelf. Certainly there should be flowers in the home as well as on the superintendent's table and the secretary's desk. The visiting parakeet or canary may be used in the home rather than on the nature shelf.

Sunday school, Training Union, Church Music, and Sunbeam leadership may need to plan together for the nature materials that will be used. Otherwise, each group should put their materials away after each session.

2. *Suggested Activities and Guidance*

Nature materials are used to teach about God rather than as an end in themselves. When tadpoles were first brought to Jimmy's department, he remarked to his daddy, "My teacher said that God would change those tadpoles into frogs, but I don't think he can." Jimmy's concept of God was greatly increased each Sunday as he hurried to the aquarium to see the development that had taken place.

Just placing the nature materials on the shelf will not guarantee that the child will have challenging experiences, however. Two principles should be kept in mind:

(1) All workers in the department should be familiar with the nature materials in the room and should be able to answer the child's questions about them. Some questions will not be anticipated and must be answered with, "I don't know, but I will try to find out and tell you next Sunday." Such questions as the following can be anticipated, however, and workers should be prepared to answer them: How did the hornets make this nest? Can the snail get out of that shell? How are bricks made? What made that grow? One worker may be asked to do needed research and share the information with others at a teachers' meeting.

(2) Children's interest corresponds with *their* activity rather than with the teacher's activity. A beautiful floral arrangement by a teacher may go unnoticed, but the flowers the child arranged in chicken wire in a foil-covered coffee can will be very meaningful to him. A bottle garden made by a teacher sat in a window for a year without a child ever commenting on it. One made by the children themselves was inspected every week. The potted plant brought and cared for by the teacher will not be as interesting to the children as the one they help to plant and water.

The outdoors should be a part of the teaching area whenever it is at all practical. In some sections of the country

it may be worthwhile to have a part or all of the sessions outside on some Sundays.

3. *Values of These Experiences*

Children may be led to feel awe and reverence when they see the things God does every day.

A group of five-year-olds had gone for a walk on a spring morning. Soon they found (as the teacher had known they would) some seeds that looked like airplanes.

"Where did they come from?" they asked.

"Let's see if we can find out," the teacher said.

They walked to the next block, where they found a tree covered with the "airplanes." The children were amazed that the seed had traveled so far. The teacher reminded them that the wind had been blowing hard that week. "I think God must have planned for these seeds to be ready to fall in March, when the wind blows most," she said.

The children were unusually quiet for a few moments, then Jim said reverently, "Isn't God remarkable?"

The child comes to understand more fully how God provides for us when he sees such products as wool and yarn and cloth or wheat and flour and bread.

Bible verses such as the following, and many others, come alive through their association with nature experiences:

"God . . . careth for you" (1 Peter 5:5–7).

"God . . . hath made every thing beautiful" (Eccl. 3:10–11).

"God saw every thing that he had made, and . . . it was very good" (Gen. 1:31).

"God . . . causeth the grass to grow" (Psalm 104:1–14).

"The flowers appear on the earth; the time of the singing of birds is come" (Song of Sol. 2:12).

Nature materials may give a child a feeling of security. Debby carried the horned toad in a little screen wire box until she felt secure in the room. Buff dried his tears only when he became interested in watching the fish.

Bring the fascinating world of nature into your room and watch for the new teaching opportunities you will find.

IV. TEACHING THROUGH BLOCKS

Children like to build things. Activities involving construction are popular with many children and are rated among the most worthwhile by many teachers.

1. *Materials You May Use*

Large building blocks should have an important place in activity time each Sunday. Along with the blocks, figures of families, community helpers, and barnyard animals will be used from time to time. (The figures may be mounted on plywood, cardboard, or starched cotton cloth and cut out.) Miniature home and church furniture may be included. Soft plastic transportation toys and farm implements are frequently suggested for use.

2. *Suggested Activities and Guidance*

Teachers can influence the child's interest and, to some extent, predetermine his activities by the materials they make available. If a paper doll family and the home furniture are on the shelf, the children will probably build a house. However, if their interest lies in another direction, teachers will recognize the values in whatever the child is doing. Only when the child can think of nothing to build, or when his building is not acceptable, should the teacher suggest what he will build.

3. *Values of These Experiences*

There are many values in block play. As in most other activities, the child can be led to relate Bible teaching to his own life as he works and plays with others. He sees the value of being kind and helpful and loving.

The first signs of progress in working together may come as Beginners use blocks. Children who have just been promoted from a Nursery department often work independently. There may be five barns being built in front of the block shelf. If there is only one tractor for the five barns, the children may argue over who should have it. Patient, understanding teachers recognize that these arguments are a part of growth, and will often let the children work them out alone (meanwhile observing closely the indications of further teaching needed). By the time the children leave the five-year department, most of them will have learned from experience that working together to build one big barn is more rewarding than working separately.

Children have many opportunities to solve problems as they build with blocks. One group, who would soon be entering school, was building a schoolhouse. Chuck came to the teacher asking that she borrow some long blocks from another room, since they did not have enough for their roof. The teacher explained to Chuck that other groups were using their blocks, and suggested that he try to find another way to finish the roof.

From the corner of her eye she watched the progress. Scotty suggested tearing the building down and building something else, but Chuck insisted that they could find a solution. As they discussed and eliminated a number of suggestions, each child seemed to be thinking through the problem carefully. The teacher offered no suggestions.

Finally a solution occurred to one of the group. They could build an inside wall through the middle of the building and two short blocks could be used for each section of the roof. Each of the children glowed with achievement when the teacher was called to see the finished building. Many experiences such as this will help them to form the habit of solving problems instead of quitting when problems arise.

Like other materials, blocks provide testing for teaching. Who shares? Who insists upon having his way? Who will not work with others? The child often reveals his needs as he works (or refuses to work) with the group.

The wise use of interwoven materials may relate experiences with blocks (or any other material) to any of the teaching objectives discussed in chapter 3.

FOR CLASS DISCUSSION

1. Observe a group of children at play, either in the home or church. How many different situations did they play? How did they determine what they would do next? Was one child a leader for the entire group? Did they ever "run out of ideas" of what to play next?

2. Select one of the activities discussed in this chapter. Refer to the list of objectives in chapter 3 and mark all of those objectives which can be achieved to a significant extent through the activity you have selected. Consider your use of this activity in your own department. How can you relate it more closely to the objectives you have checked?

FOR FURTHER STUDY

Dillard, Polly Hargis. *The Church Kindergarten*. Nashville: Broadman Press, 1958. Chap. 7.

Ruth E. Hartley, Lawrence K. Frank, Robert M. Goldenson. *Understanding Children's Play*. New York: Columbia University Press, 1952. Chaps. 3, 4.

Read, Katherine H. *The Nursery School*. Chap. 11.

CHAPTER 5

I. TEACHING THROUGH BOOKS
   1. Materials Which May Be Used
   2. Suggested Activities and Guidance
   3. Values of These Experiences

II. TEACHING THROUGH ART MATERIALS
   1. Materials Which May Be Used
   2. Suggested Activities and Guidance
   3. Values of These Experiences

III. TEACHING THROUGH PUZZLES
   1. Materials Which May Be Used
   2. Suggested Activities and Guidance
   3. Values of These Experiences

IV. TEACHING THROUGH RECORDINGS
   1. Materials Which May Be Used
   2. Suggested Activities and Guidance
   3. Values of These Experiences

V. TEACHING THROUGH USE OF SPECIAL ACTIVITIES
   1. Piano
   2. Other Materials

VI. PLANNING FOR ACTIVITY TEACHING

5

Teaching Through Activities
[*Continued*]

IN the preceding chapter learning through three types of materials was discussed. Others are presented in this chapter.

I. TEACHING THROUGH BOOKS

The bookrack with well-selected books is a favorite section of the room for some four- and five-year-olds.

1. *Materials Which May Be Used*

Curriculum materials contain suggested lists of books correlated with the teaching emphasis. Many of these books are available through church or public libraries. Keep in mind the following principles:

Choose books that contribute to the desired outcome of the unit or lesson.

Choose books that have good art work. (We eliminate a book because of even one objectionable picture.)

Choose books that have few unfamiliar words or ideas.

Choose books that are realistic. (Avoid those in which animals wear clothes or talk to people.)

Choose books which relate experiences similar to those which the children have had and use characters with whom they can identify.

Choose books that will lead to religious experiences for the children. (Many books not religious in content can be related to spiritual truths.)

2. *Suggested Activities and Guidance*

The child may select a book from the shelf and sit in a nearby chair or on the floor. He may look at the pictures alone or with another child, or tell the story to another child if he has seen the book before.

Sometimes a teacher may be asked to join a group to read a story. If the book is very long, she will tell the story in her own words rather than reading it directly. Frequently she will need to change a word to make the book more meaningful to the child. For example, we use many excellent books from publishers who use the term "kindergarten department" to designate the room for four's and five's in Sunday school. Since this term would have no meaning for our children, the teacher will read "Sunday school room" instead.

3. *Values of These Experiences*

Books give a child an opportunity to work alone when he does not feel like being with a group. Every child needs this experience of being alone from time to time.

Children learn much from books. Such stories as the "Basic Science Series" will give answers to many of the child's nature questions, and the teacher may relate the information to God. The "I Want to Be" books will help the child to appreciate some of God's helpers and the work they do. *Sunday with Stevie* and *Jimmy Goes to Church* help him to make adjustments as he enters the four-year age group. Some children's books, such as *I Know God Loves Me* and *The Little Old Lady* teach specific spiritual or Bible truths.

Markets are crowded with children's books—some good, some bad. Introduce your children to good books, and you will greatly enrich their lives.

II. TEACHING THROUGH ART MATERIALS

One of the first activities introduced into children's work in our churches was the use of art materials.

1. *Materials Which May Be Used*

Crayons are usually the first—and sometimes the only—material provided. The well-equipped department for four's and five's will contain the following art materials:

For easel painting—A double easel, newsprint, tempera paints, long-handled brushes with ¾-inch bristles, smocks (made from men's shirts), sponges

For finger painting—Slick-finish paper or plastic-top tables, sponges, smocks, plastic aprons, commercial finger paint or homemade paint

The following recipe may be used: 1 pint prepared starch, ¾ cup soap flakes (not detergent), ¼ cup talcum powder, ½ teaspoon oil of cloves. Whip soap flakes into starch with rotary beater. When thoroughly mixed, add talcum powder and oil of cloves. Store in airtight jar, and add dry tempera when ready to use. If thin paint is desired, add tempera to liquid starch and omit the other ingredients.

For freehand work—Manila paper for drawing, large

crayons, colored construction paper, pieces of colored cloth, blunt scissors, paste, well-selected magazine or leaflet pictures

For clay modeling—Clay (not to be confused with play dough), smocks, sponges, plastic aprons, clay boards about 12 by 18 inches (not needed if tables have plastic tops)

Other special materials will be used from time to time.

2. *Suggested Activities and Guidance*

A child may need some guidance in how to use art materials. Certain limits will need to be set and maintained.

(1) *Painting.*—In easel painting, the teacher will set up the easel, clip the paper on if the children cannot reach the clips easily, and mix the paints. What the child decides to paint and the colors he chooses will be entirely his decision.

When a child first uses paints, he will experiment with line and color and will likely not paint anything specific. To him, it is "a picture," and that is that. Insisting that he tell what he is painting only frustrates him. After a period of time, he may begin to paint airplanes or trucks or flowers or houses—whatever he is interested in at the moment. (A few children may have reached this stage even before coming to a four-year department; others may not reach it until Primary age.)

SEE WHAT I MADE!

Joyce, newly a lover of the art of painting,
Stood squarely.
High before her stood the easel,
Wide before her stretched the paper.
Just last week straight lines had charmed her.
Looking at her morning's work, she named it:
"This is a picture of stripes."
Now her brush swept round in circles,
One beside another standing.
"This is a picture of Dora's mother,"
Murmured Joyce, creating gladly.
"No, it doesn't look like a mother.
"See what I made!
"It's a bicycle." [1]

The wise teacher will not ask what the child is painting. She will recognize that he usually paints *feelings* instead of *things*. She will not comment on how well or how poorly he has done. Her remarks may be something like this:

"You're having fun painting, aren't you?"

"I like the colors you are using."

"God must like those colors, too. He used blue like yours when he made the sky and green like yours when he made the grass. Can you think of some way God used yellow like yours?" Thus the manipulative activity of painting may become the setting for an experience of worship.

(2) *Using crayons.*—The art shelf will usually contain materials from which a child may choose those in which he is interested. One Sunday he may choose to draw a picture

[1] Ruth Wendell Washburn, *Children Know Their Friends* (New York: William Morrow and Co., Inc., 1949), p. 99.

with crayons on manila paper. Because his arm muscles and his eye muscles are not ready for intricate work, we will never give him paper smaller than 12 by 18 inches. We will not give him small crayons, nor outline pictures to be colored. The child will draw whatever he wishes. Often the younger child will experiment with drawing lines or coloring without any attempt at making a picture.

(3) *Cutting and pasting.*—Some children may be interested in cutting pictures from old leaflets or magazines and pasting them on construction paper or cardboard. They may make pictures from construction paper or cloth and mount them on paper. In either case, let the ideas be the child's. The teacher may make suggestions about the use of the sponge to wipe off paste or where to put the scraps of paper, but what goes into the picture is the child's idea entirely.

(4) *Using clay.*—If a child wishes to use clay, he should wear a smock and a plastic apron. If there are no tables with plastic tops, clay boards will be needed. The child may pound and hit his clay and mold it as he wishes. Usually, the clay will be returned to the container (a crock with lid) when the child has finished. In a few instances the objects may be set aside to dry.

(5) *Finger painting.*—Like clay, finger paint will be used only occasionally in most departments. It is an especially good activity for a tense, nervous child. Let the child wear a smock covered by a plastic apron. Children stand while finger painting.

If a child is to paint directly on a plastic-top table, the teacher may put a dab of the paint mixture in front of him and let him add the powdered tempera for color. The tempera may be kept in salt shakers for easy use. The child may paint with both hands on the table top. When he has finished, he will wipe the paint off with a wet sponge, rinsing as many times as necessary to clean the table.

If paper is being used, it should be wiped with a damp

sponge before the paint is applied. If the child wishes to take his picture home, set it aside to dry. In damp climates it may be necessary to wait until the following Sunday to give the picture to the child.

(6) *Special projects.*—From time to time there may be special art activities which will be initiated and directed by the teacher. These should be used only occasionally, and the children should have a part in making plans. Ideas for such projects should be presented in group time the Sunday before they are to be started.

The superintendent might say: "Mrs. Short told me that some of the children in the hospital do not have picture books. We have many pictures that could be pasted in scrapbooks. Can you think of something we could do for the sick children who have no books?"

When the children have made the desired suggestions, the superintendent might continue: "Mrs. Short, would you help us with that next Sunday? All of the children who want to make scrapbooks can help you. If there is not enough room for all next Sunday, others could work with you some other time. Would you get the pages for the books and have the pictures ready for the boys and girls to paste?"

There are other activities of this type. Friezes may be made of long strips of wrapping paper fastened to the wall with masking tape. The frieze is prepared by pasting, painting, or drawing a series of pictures related to the unit emphasis. There may be special holiday projects, such as painting seed pods for Christmas decorations or making Mother's Day cards. Rarely, if ever, should there be an art activity in which every child is asked to make the same thing at the same time. Even in making Christmas or Mother's Day gifts, the child should have the privilege of choosing from several things, or doing something else if he prefers.

3. *Values of These Experiences*

The value and appeal of art activities will be determined largely by the amount of initiative the children are allowed in the use of the materials. There is little value in an activity where the child puts the finishing touches on something started by a teacher, or makes something by following detailed instructions.

In the book *Children Know Their Friends,* Ruth Wendell Washburn says:

When a five-year-old says he does not know how to paint a boat, the unthinking adult says, "You do it thus or so." The adult with time and wisdom says, "Here are three books in which there are pictures of boats. We can find the kind of boat you want to paint and then you can see how much you want to try to put in your picture.[2]

Creative experiences (when the child decides what he wants to make and how he will make it) will not result in perfect or near-perfect products, but there is no place for

[2] *Ibid.,* p. 151.

"handwork displays" in work with four's and five's. The process and how the child feels about it are more important than the product. When we provide opportunities for a little child to work creatively, we are enriching his life now and helping him to become a creative adult.

Easel and finger painting are relaxing and are experiences where the child works alone quietly. Both of these factors make them valuable activities for the child who is tense or upset when he enters the room. Until he has relaxed from his tensions, the child is not ready for the spiritual truths we wish to help him learn.

Painting or drawing often helps a child who is lacking in self-confidence. Having his picture accepted and given no more or less recognition than pictures by other children helps the child to feel accepted.

Painting, drawing, or pounding clay are acceptable ways of working out bad feelings and expressing good feelings. As a result of unhappy experiences, everyone—adult and child alike—has bad feelings from time to time. These may be expressed in undesirable ways, such as kicking down someone's block building or "yelling" at someone. Or, the feelings may find outlets through such channels as painting or working with clay. When bad feelings are not expressed, personality difficulties occur. Good, happy feelings may be expressed through art materials, also.

One five-year-old, who was having difficulty adjusting to his home situation (and, as a result, to Sunday school) after the birth of the third little brother, found painting a substitute for temper tantrums. When he entered the room in a bad mood, he invariably painted a black picture, which he described as a picture of a storm. After the painting experience, he seemed to relax and could join a group of children for happy experiences together.

The use of art materials provides opportunities to learn

to share and take turns. Since most departments will provide only one double easel, the children must learn to take turns using it. "Susan and Billy are painting now and Tim has asked to paint next. I will write your name on this paper we taped on the wall. As soon as it is your turn, I will call you. You may work somewhere else while you are waiting."

The child learns that he may not paint before his turn, but that he may depend on the teacher to see that he has his turn. Because his thoughts about God are closely associated with his teacher, the child unconsciously associates the idea of dependability which he experiences in his teacher with his concept of God.

Usually it is best to limit such materials as crayons, scissors, or paste sticks so that the children will have experiences in taking turns and sharing. We are not being kind to the children when we provide enough materials for each one so that there will be no disputes. Children learn to take turns by having experiences in taking turns. Learning to share and take turns means learning to think of others instead of oneself —a basic concept for Christian character.

Art projects which are teacher directed and teacher initiated have less value than the child-initiated experiences. Some value in these special activities may come from the satisfaction of making something to be shared or from the conversation about the projects during the time the children are working on them. Such projects should be used only rarely, in contrast to the every-Sunday opportunities to do freehand work.

The child's concept of himself, which is so important in the Christian experience, will be affected greatly by the satisfaction he receives from his creative efforts. Many Bible truths may be taught at a later date if they are not learned now, but the self-concept formed in the early years of life is seldom changed.

III. Teaching Through Puzzles

Another teaching material which may be used effectively with four's and five's is inlaid puzzles.

1. *Materials Which May Be Used*

Wooden inlay puzzles are usually recommended, but when they are not available, cardboard puzzles may be used. However, the durability of wooden puzzles often makes them less expensive in the long run. Homemade puzzles (suitable pictures glued to pieces of plywood or corrugated cardboard and cut into pieces) are often satisfactory.

A picture illustrating a Bible story should not be used for a puzzle. Just as we do not mutilate a Bible or a Bible story, we do not cut up a picture representing a Bible character. Neither is it wise to use unrealistic pictures, such as cars or busses with faces, or animals wearing clothes. Suitable puzzle pictures are fruits, vegetables, milk, community helpers (such as doctor, milkman, or bus driver), flowers, birds, or realistic animals.

Puzzles should not have very small pieces, not only be-

cause they may be lost easily but also because the child's muscles have not developed sufficiently for handling small details without undue tension. The number of pieces will vary with the age of the children. Younger four's will usually need puzzles with about twelve pieces, while most five's can work more difficult puzzles.

2. Suggested Activities and Guidance

The child who wishes to work a puzzle may select it from the puzzle rack or shelf and take it to the designated table. He will take the pieces out one at a time (instead of dumping them all out on the table) and place them on his left side. In this way, they are not mixed with pieces of other puzzles being used at the same time, and (incidentally) the child is forming the habit of left-to-right eye movement, so important in reading.

If a child needs help, another child may offer assistance. "I'll be glad to help you if you like," a friendly teacher may say to a child having difficulty. Her help should consist of suggestions, however, and rarely, if ever, should a teacher put a piece in place for a child.

"This piece looks like the cow's leg. Where do you suppose it belongs?" or, "The car needs a wheel. Do you see a piece that looks like a wheel?"

When the child has finished a puzzle, he puts it back on the puzzle rack.

3. Values of These Experiences

A puzzle provides an opportunity for a child to work alone when he prefers. The child receives a feeling of achievement when he has worked a puzzle "all by himself," thus growing in self-confidence.

He learns to take turns and share. There is only one dog puzzle and each child must wait his turn to use it.

Because we insist upon a child finishing (with help, if

necessary) a puzzle which he starts, he makes progress toward learning the habit of finishing each task before moving on to something else. (If everyone formed this habit in childhood, our church programs would not be held back by people who accept responsibilities, then drop out.)

A well-selected puzzle often serves as a springboard for conversation between the worker and child. For example, during a missionary unit the airplane puzzle was placed on the rack. As Sally worked it, she told the teacher about a trip she had made by plane. "Some of the money we brought to Sunday school this morning will be used to help buy a plane ticket," the teacher said, and described some work in which missionaries traveled by plane.

IV. TEACHING THROUGH RECORDINGS

Within recent years, record players and recordings have become popular in children's departments in our churches.

1. Materials Which May Be Used

A portable player (three speed) with a good tone is desirable. Curriculum materials and your *Baptist Book Store Catalog* list suitable records.

2. Suggested Activities and Guidance

The teachers will select the records suitable for each Sunday and place them on the table or in the record cabinet. The child may then select a record and play it as he chooses, provided he follows such rules as the teachers may find it necessary to make. A teacher may join the child in listening to the records or in conversation about the music, as she sees fit.

3. Values of These Experiences

The teaching value of music for young children has long been recognized. If the records are well chosen, the child's appreciation of music will be strengthened, and his thinking will be stimulated. Many behavior patterns are taught through suitable songs, such as "A Helper I Will Be" or "Love One Another."

The child has opportunities to learn to share as he plays records. Disputes frequently arise over who plays the next record. With necessary guidance from teachers, these disputes often are steps in learning to take turns.

Listening to records is a relaxing experience for many children. For others, the experience of selecting and playing records themselves builds up self-confidence. Like books, recordings may be good or bad, so the values which the child receives will largely be determined by the records selected. A wise choice will result in experiences related to many of the objectives listed in chapter 3.

V. Teaching Through Use of Special Activities

In addition to these regular activities discussed in this chapter and the previous one, there are special activities which will be used from time to time.

1. *Piano*

Children are fascinated by the piano and may be allowed to experiment with using it themselves during activity time, if they can remember that only one person plays at a time, only one key is played at a time, and that they touch the keys very softly.

On other occasions the piano may be used for a teacher-directed activity, with the teacher playing suitable songs for the children to identify or to sing. Some children may enjoy gathering around the piano to sing.

2. *Autoharp*

The autoharp is a relatively inexpensive musical instrument. It may be used in addition to, or (in cases where budgets and/or space are limited) instead of, a piano. The twelve-chord model is adequate for Beginner departments.

No musical training is required to play an autoharp. Chords are marked on the instrument buttons and also on many of the songs in *Songs for 4's and 5's*. During activity time, a worker may press the chord buttons and let the children take turns strumming the string to accompany their singing.

3. *Other Materials*

During various emphases throughout the year other special activities may be planned. These are usually suggested in curriculum materials.

For example, a hospital or doctor's office is often set up when there is an emphasis on community helpers or on missions. A doctor's kit may be secured from a toy department, or one may be assembled by the workers. Usually a stethoscope, playlike hypodermic needle, bandages, pill boxes, and bottles are used. Simple doctor and nurse uniforms are often used.

These materials may be used in the homeliving area if there is no other room, but children today are much more accustomed to seeing doctors in their offices than at home. Occasionally doll beds may be borrowed and a hospital set up. Nurses' caps may be made from paper, and dolls (or children, if beds are sturdy) may become patients.

From such experiences the children learn an appreciation of doctors and nurses as God's helpers. They learn kindness toward people who are sick, and, many times, they become interested in the work of medical missionaries.

Other activities may be added as they relate to special emphases.

VI. PLANNING FOR ACTIVITY TEACHING

Teachers' books are teaching tools. The activity suggestions which they carry are planned to help workers provide meaningful experiences for the children during activity time. Not every activity is practical for every church. Workers should consider the needs of children and the limitations of space and equipment and adapt the suggestions as they see fit.

Preparation for teaching should begin with the reading of all the material for the unit before the teachers' meeting preceding the first Sunday. Before each weekly officers and teachers' meeting each worker should read carefully the materials for the following Sunday and review unit activities. She should make notes of ideas which come to her mind or questions to be considered by the group.

At the meetings, whether monthly or weekly, each worker should be prepared to participate. A thorough study of the lesson (or lessons) is necessary if the planning is to be worthwhile. Frequently the superintendent will ask certain workers to accept special assignments.

During the lesson planning period such questions as the following should be considered: What materials can we use next week to stimulate the desired experience? Where are these materials available (if they are not already in the department)? What is the responsibility of each teacher for next Sunday?

Worthwhile learning experiences do not just happen. Study and planning are essential.

FOR CLASS DISCUSSION

1. Examine a group of books suggested for use with Beginners in Sunday school (see *Beginner Teacher*). Compare them with the objectives for the Beginner years. To which objective is each book most closely related?

2. In a class period you may wish to divide into eight groups for a "buzz session." Each group will be asked to consider one of the activity areas discussed in chapter 4 or 5 and to list the objectives (see chap. 3) which that activity can be used to achieve to a significant degree.

FOR FURTHER STUDY

Dillard, Polly Hargis. *The Church Kindergarten*. Chap. 4.

Hartley, Ruth Edith, *et al. Understanding Children's Play*.

Heinz, Mamie W. *Growing and Learning in the Kindergarten*. Chap. 4.

Read, Katherine H. *The Nursery School*. Chap. 12.

CHAPTER 6

I. USING THE BIBLE
  1. To Interpret Experiences
  2. To Solve Problems
  3. To Recall Previous Teachings

II. USING MUSIC IN ACTIVITY TIME
  1. To Strengthen Teaching
  2. To Solve Problems
  3. To Express Feelings
  4. To Deepen Appreciations

III. USING PICTURES
  1. To Interpret Experiences
  2. To Stimulate Interest
  3. To Deepen Appreciations

IV. USING CONVERSATION
  1. To Redirect Undesirable Activities
  2. To Meet Individual Needs
  3. To Encourage Special Interests

V. USING RELAXATION

VI. SOME DANGERS IN INTERWOVEN ACTIVITIES

6

Interwoven Activities

WHAT does the teacher do during activity time? In addition to giving routine guidance (see chap. 7) she is to enrich the experiences for the child. This enrichment will take place whenever the teacher sees an opportunity to interpret an experience for the child or to make it more meaningful for him. For this purpose she will use what have been designated as "interwoven activities." The term denotes the use of enrichment materials—the Bible, music, pictures, conversation—which are interwoven with the child's activities in order to give him experiences with spiritual truths.

The use of interwoven materials is determined by the child's actions and responses. The teacher must be thoroughly familiar with the enrichment materials and alert at all times to recognize opportunities for their use.

I. USING THE BIBLE

Every worker (including the secretary) should bring and use her Bible during activity time. Some Sundays the department Bible (1450BP) may be on the nature shelf, opened to a suitable picture. On other Sundays it may be on the chest of drawers, available for use in the home, on the table used for puzzles, or near the bookrack.

1. *To Interpret Experiences*

As Scotty came into the department one morning, he was greeted by Mrs. Bruton, the secretary. He dropped his offering in the basket, and Mrs. Bruton opened her Bible to 2 Corinthians 1:24 and read, "We . . . are helpers."

"I'm glad you were a helper this morning, Scotty. Some of the money you brought will be used to help pay Lucy for cleaning our room. Some of it will be used to help buy bricks to build a church for some people who have no place to go to Sunday school."

Scotty walked to the record player. With two other children, he took turns playing records. When they played "Happy Sunday Morning," the children sang with the record. Mr. Emmett heard the singing and joined them. Opening his Bible to Psalm 9:11, he said: "You are doing just what this verse says. Can you guess what it is?"

The children made several guesses, none of them correct. "Right here I read, 'Sing praises,'" he told them, "I'm glad you are singing praise songs this morning." Mr. Emmett moved on to another area.

2. *To Solve Problems*

At Jerry's invitation, Scotty left the record player to help build a barn for the wooden animals. After a few minutes Douglas and Katie joined Jerry and Scotty and asked for some blocks to build an airplane hangar. Jerry and Scotty refused to give them any, and a heated argument followed. Mrs. Hughes stepped in just in time to prevent Katie from hitting Scotty with one of the large blocks.

"Scotty and Jerry want to build a barn with the blocks. Douglas and Katie want to use them, too. Can you think of anything we could do?" There was no response.

"When I don't know what I should do, sometimes I read the Bible to find out what is best." Opening her Bible to Ephesians 4:32, Mrs. Hughes read, "Be ye kind." Turning to 1 John 4:7, she read, "Love one another."

"Does this help you to think of a way we could all be happy together?" she asked.

The children were quiet for a moment, then Scotty suggested enthusiastically, "Let's all build a big airplane hangar, and we can give the farm animals a plane ride!"

3. *To Recall Previous Teachings*

Mrs. Hughes left them to join Linda and Mark at the bookrack. Mark was "reading" a story to Linda. Both noticed the ribbon markers in Mrs. Hughes' Bible.

"Let me find the verses," Linda said eagerly.

"Me, too," Mark added.

Taking turns, they found the marked verses (those which had been used during the past few Sundays) and read them with Mrs. Hughes. As they finished, Carol joined them. "Let's play the 'I remember' game," she suggested.

Carol was asked to be first and she said, "I remember about a baby whose mother put him in a basket in the river. Who was he?" The other children took turns, and the game lasted until cleanup time.

Mr. Wynn noticed that Nelle was standing in front of the aquarium, very interested in the new fish which had been added that week. He joined her, his Bible in his hand. They talked about the fish for some time.

"I remember a story about fish that Mrs. Lane told us one Sunday. Do you?" Nelle could not remember. Mr. Wynn opened his Bible to Genesis 1 and read, "In the beginning God created the heaven and the earth." He pointed out the verse that says God made the stars and the moon. He touched the verses which tell that God made fish. They talked about some of the other things mentioned in the story.

"Daddy read that to me out of our Bible," Nelle told Mr. Wynn, as Mrs. Lane called them to group time.

II. USING MUSIC IN ACTIVITY TIME

Every worker should sing with the children at some time on Sunday morning. She need not be a trained soloist and, if she feels insecure, she may sing so softly that only the child nearest her will hear.

1. To Strengthen Teaching

The secretary may sing as the child drops his money in the offering basket:

My Money

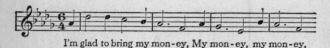

I'm glad to bring my mon-ey, My mon-ey, my mon-ey,

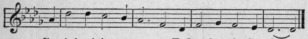

I'm glad to bring my mon-ey To Sun-day school to-day.

Adapted from words by Mattie C. Leatherwood. Music by B. B. McKinney. From *Songs We Sing*, Broadman Press, 1939.

On another Sunday she may sing the second stanza of "We Are Happy Children" or "I Will Tell."

2. To Solve Problems

Jean was overstimulated as she arrived, and on the verge of tears. Her high-pitched voice revealed her tensions.

"Let's listen to a new record together," the teacher said. They sat by the record player and listened to a recording of hymns played on the organ. Jean relaxed and in a few minutes was ready for other activities.

Nancy and Bob were working puzzles. Nancy suddenly decided she wanted the puzzle Bob was using and suggested that they exchange. Bob refused, and Nancy attempted to take his puzzle by force. A teacher who was nearby acted as if she did not see the trouble, but began to sing:

> Share with one another,
> Share with one another,
> This is the happy way,
> Share with one another.
>
> MATTIE C. LEATHERWOOD, *Songs We Sing*

Both children looked up when she began to sing. The teacher pretended to be busy with a book, but continued to hum the song. After a moment, Nancy released her hold on the puzzle pieces she was clutching and said quietly, "May I have it when you are through?"

Denny and Jimmy were working in the kitchen making cherry pies from play dough, while David looked on.

"Could I have some dough?" David asked.

"We're using all of it," Jimmy answered.

Denny hesitated for a moment and then gave David a very small piece—enough for one cherry but not for a pie.

A teacher standing nearby turned so that she could see what was going on without the children's being conscious that she was watching. She began to sing softly:

> How do friendly children play?
> I know, I know.
> They share their blocks and share their toys
> With other little girls and boys
> Because it is the happy way,
> I know, I know.
>
> MATTIE C. LEATHERWOOD, *Songs We Sing*

Before she had finished singing, Jimmy had given more than half of his dough to David, and Denny shared with Jimmy. The teacher, realizing that personal satisfaction is a much better reward than commendation, did not acknowledge that she had seen the episode.

At cleanup time no one was interested in putting away

the blocks, although Philip, Karen, Janice, and Lester had used them at various times during the morning. Philip picked up one or two and then decided to arrange the chairs for group time. Karen and Janice each put one or two blocks on the shelf and then found another job. A teacher walked to the shelf and began to sing as she stacked the blocks:

> I'll put away the blocks,
> Won't you come help me?
> And we will be church helpers,
> Don't you see.
> Adapted from "A Little Helper"
> MATTIE C. LEATHERWOOD, *Songs We Sing*

Lester, Philip, Janice, and Karen joined her immediately and soon all the blocks were neatly stacked on the shelf.

3. *To Express Feelings*

Lynn went to the easel to paint, and seemed to be enjoying the experience thoroughly. A teacher, who realized what a happy time she was having, sang to a made-up tune:

> Lynn is painting, painting, painting,
> Painting is such fun.

Lynn and the teacher exchanged friendly smiles, and the teacher moved on to another group.

Marlean came in one Sunday morning and obviously looked for a place where she could be alone. No one was in the homeliving corner, so she sat down in the rocking chair. She turned her chair toward the wall so that her back would be toward the other children as they arrived.

The workers had placed Ortlip's picture of Jesus on the wall in the home that morning. When Marlean turned away from the other children, she was sitting directly in front of the picture. For about five minutes she sat very still, look-ing at the picture and smiling. A teacher who had been observing her all the time stepped to her side and sang softly, with Marlean joining:

> Oh, how I love Jesus,
> Oh, how I love Jesus.
> Oh, how I love Jesus,
> Because he first loved me.
>
> FREDERICK WHITFIELD

When they had finished singing, Marlean turned to the teacher and smiled. "He loves me," she said.

4. *To Deepen Appreciations*

Sammye brought a bowl of autumn leaves when she came to Sunday school one October morning. As they arranged the leaves, the teacher and Sammye sang:

> Fall is here,
> Fall is here;
> The red leaves tell us
> Fall is here.
>
> AURORA M. SHUMATE, *Songs Children Sing*

Sammye told about a drive into the country to get the leaves.

> God's beautiful world,
> God's beautiful world,
> I love God's beautiful world.
> He made it for you,
> He made it for me,
> I love God's beautiful world.
>
> AURORA M. SHUMATE, *Songs We Sing*

Sammye began that song spontaneously, and the teacher joined her in singing it.

"I'm so glad God made the world so pretty," Sammye said.

"Let's sing 'We Thank You, God,'" the teacher said. "We could sing the words 'We thank you, God, for autumn leaves.'" Sammye and the teacher bowed their heads and sang their prayer—just a few feet from a group building with blocks and another group working puzzles.

III. USING PICTURES

Beginner teaching pictures provide a wide selection of pictures for every occasion. Many teachers also clip and file magazine pictures suitable for use in the department.

1. *To Interpret Experiences*

As Tommy entered the room one morning he saw on Miss King's table a picture of a man. When he dropped his offering in the basket, he asked, "Who is that man?"

Miss King replied: "I'm glad you brought an offering this morning, Tommy, because some of it will be sent to this man. His name is Mr. Smith, and he is a missionary. He has two little boys. Mr. and Mrs. Smith and the little boys live in South America, and they go to many towns where people do not know about Jesus. Some of our offerings are used to buy gas for their car and to build churches for people who do not have any. I found this picture in a magazine, and I wanted you to know about the Smiths.

"We bring our money because we love Jesus, and we want to help Mr. and Mrs. Smith and all the other missionaries tell other people about him."

2. *To Stimulate Interest*

Tommy walked to the block shelf and found a picture of a hospital on the wall nearby. He looked at it for a few minutes. There was an ambulance near the hospital. On the shelf with the blocks Tommy found the plastic ambulance and the doctor and nurse from the set of block figures. Tommy put them on the floor and began to take blocks from the shelf to build a hospital.

Elaine and Martha were not interested in doing anything and had succeeded in disturbing several groups.

"I need someone to play a picture game with me," Miss Betty said. "Would you hold these pictures, Martha?"

One at a time, Miss Betty took the pictures from Martha. "I remember a Bible friend. This friend shared something with Jesus. Can you tell me about this picture?"

Martha, Elaine, and Kyle, when he joined them later, took turns describing the pictures.

3. *To Deepen Appreciations*

During a unit on thanking God for his love and care, workers placed in the room each Sunday pictures illustrating different ways God cares for us. One Sunday they used food pictures. Pictures of a bakery scene, of fruits, vegetables, and milk were arranged in various places.

Marla and Ken joined Mr. Parker to tell him about an experience they had during the previous week. After sharing the experience, they remained and "visited" with him. Mr. Parker sensed that they wanted his attention, so he said, "I see a picture of something God planned for me. The farmer helped me to have it. He plants seeds, and God makes them grow. Can you find the picture?"

Marla then described another picture and let Mr. Parker and Ken find it.

IV. USING CONVERSATION

"Just talking" may be one of the greatest teaching opportunities a teacher has. Conversation may be used in many ways.

1. *To Redirect Undesirable Activities*

A teacher heard a shriek from the playlike home, where a combination hospital and home had been set up. Hurrying to the scene, she found that Kenneth was holding the doll up by her feet. "I'm the witch doctor," he said. "I'm going to kill this baby and cook her."

"I'm another witch doctor," said Sam, holding the broom. "This is my poison stick. Everyone I touch drops dead."

The teacher breathed a prayer for guidance in handling a difficult situation. "You must be having fun," she said. "Did you know that there are really people who believe in witch doctors?"

The children seemed interested, so she continued: "Some missionary friends of mine told me about witch doctors in Africa. They dress in funny clothes and paint their faces. They do strange things to make sick people well, but they can't really help them. When witch doctors learn to love Jesus, they stop being witch doctors. They know that God helps doctors and nurses to help people get well, but that witch doctors can't help them."

"It's all right for me to be a witch doctor," Sam said. "I've never heard about Jesus."

"What could we do about that?" the teacher asked.

"I'll be a missionary and go to Africa and tell him about Jesus," Kenneth said. He began to pack his doctor kit for the trip.

"Oh, it's all right. I really know about Jesus. Let's just play hospital again," Sam suggested.

2. *To Meet Individual Needs*

Frequently a child wants to talk to a teacher during activity time. He may have something he really wants to share with her, or he may be seeking attention. In either case, it is important that the teacher give him her full attention. Her response will be determined by the nature of his sharing. Often he merely needs a listener, and the teacher should be as courteous in listening to him without interrupting as she would be with an adult. Usually she should sit in a child-size chair so that she will be more nearly on his level while they talk.

"We went to the fair yesterday," Jimmy said one Sunday.

"Tell me about it," the teacher said, stooping to his level.

Jimmy described in great detail a number of things he had seen. The episode was very important to Jimmy, but there seemed to be no teaching value or spiritual significance in his stories of side shows and rides. The teacher encouraged Jimmy to tell her as much as he would, however, realizing that he would not be as likely to want to take group time to talk about his experience if he had already told someone all about it.

3. *To Encourage Special Interests*

Sometimes an activity time conversation will center around questions asked by the child.

"How did the hornets make this nest?" Debby asked.

"There is a book in our library that tells about that," the teacher answered. She explained the process in simple terms so that Debby could understand.

Debby had many other questions about the hornet's nest. Many of them the teacher could answer. Her reply to the others was, "I don't know, but I'll try to find out, and we will talk about it next Sunday."

Their conversation lasted for almost ten minutes. Debby learned a great deal as a result of her curiosity about the hornet's nest she found on the nature shelf, and she was helped to recognize it as one of God's wonders.

V. USING RELAXATION

During activity time the children will be moving around a great deal, and there is not as great a need for planning specific relaxation as there is during group time. However, children may remain too long at one activity unless teachers are alert to direct their attention.

The first experience Ross had in the Beginner room after Promotion Day was one of these instances. He was very interested in puzzles, and had been taught in the Nursery department to complete a puzzle when he had started it. The teachers had accidentally left a very difficult puzzle on the rack—one that had been used by older children just before promotion. Ross selected that particular one and had started it before the teachers could divert his attention. He refused help from the older children and from the teachers, insisting that he would work it all by himself. After about thirty minutes, he was very tense and tired, but only half finished.

"Ross, I'm glad you like to finish your puzzles. Right now I need you for a few minutes. Would you mind letting Kay (an older child) finish it for you while you go with me to get a book from the library? Next time I'll let you finish your puzzle yourself, but this time I need you to help me select a book." Ross reluctantly agreed.

Some children will look at books for too long a period. Their eye muscles have not yet developed to the extent that this is good. Teachers should watch carefully to see that it does not happen. The length of time a child spends in crayon drawing should be limited also.

When a teacher sees that a child has been in one position for a period of more than ten or fifteen minutes (depending upon the age of the child) she may divert his attention in one of the following ways:

"Could you help me feed the fish?"

"Mrs. Marjorie brought us some beautiful flowers, but we need someone to arrange them. Could you do it? You will find a vase on the shelf."

"These are lovely leaves in the picture book, aren't they? As I was coming into the church, I noticed a tree with leaves that looked like that. Would you go with me outside to see if they are alike? We could take your book."

"Mrs. Gray is ready to take the offering money into the church office. Would you like to go with her?"

VI. Some Dangers in Interwoven Activities

Interwoven activities may be good or they may be weak. There are two pitfalls which children's workers should avoid: too much guidance and insufficient guidance.

Since the teacher may be with the children in one activity for the entire time in some departments, she must guard against dominating the activity. Her zeal to use Bible material may actually be harmful rather than worthwhile if she uses it in the wrong way. The teacher who tries to relate a Bible verse to everything a child says may find that he listens to none of them.

When the child is intensely interested in some worthwhile activity, it is usually best not to interrupt him. He cannot paint and listen to a Bible story at the same time. He dislikes the teacher who insists that he stop in the middle of building with blocks to hear a story, and he may associate his dislike with the Bible story itself.

The other extreme is equally dangerous. The "let alone" policy may be taken so far that the activities lose their spiritual significance. Workers may even fail to observe what is taking place and may miss the significant revelations of children's needs and interests which are to be found in every group experience.

FOR CLASS DISCUSSION

Select pictures from the picture file and "make up" a picture game which might be used during activity time.

FOR FURTHER STUDY

Heinz, Mamie W. *Growing and Learning in the Kindergarten.* Chap. 6.

CHAPTER 7

7

Using Routine Guidance

By "routine guidance" we mean the guidance which workers use over and over in directing the activities of the children. Its significant teaching values must not be overlooked.

I. In Speech and Action

In her book *The Nursery School*, Katherine H. Read gives the following guides for speech and action in handling young children:

In Speech
1. State suggestions or directions in a postive rather than a negative form.
2. Give the child a choice only when you intend to leave the situation up to him.
3. Use only words and a tone of voice which will help the child feel confident and reassured, not afraid or guilty or ashamed.
4. Avoid motivating a child by making comparisons between one child and another or encouraging competition.
5. Use your voice as a teaching tool.
6. Redirection is likely to be most effective when it is consistent with the child's own motives or interests.

In Action
7. Avoid making models in any art medium for the children to copy.
8. Give the child the minimum of help in order that he may have the maximum chance to grow in independence, but give the help the child needs.
9. Make your suggestions effective by reinforcing them when necessary.

10. The timing of a suggestion may be as important as the suggestion itself.
11. When limits are necessary, they should be clearly defined and consistently maintained.
12. Be alert to the total situation. Use the most strategic positions for supervising.
13. The health and safety of the children are a primary concern at all times.
14. Observe and take notes! [1]

Translated into work with four's and five's in Sunday school, these excellent suggestions might be used as follows:

1. Say, "Put the brush back in the jar where you found it," instead of, "Don't put the brush in another jar."

2. Don't say, "Would you like to do this?" unless you intend to let the child make his own decision. (If you say, "Don't you want to put the blocks away now?" and he says no, what will you say then?)

3. Avoid saying, "Aren't you ashamed?" or, "You were bad." You may say, "That was a bad thing for you to do."

4. Avoid saying, "Try to paint a picture that is as good as Jimmy's," or "Keep your feet still like Jimmy's."

5. Speak in a quiet voice. Always remember, "Be gentle unto all." Be firm when necessary, but never harsh. Never speak across the room to a child except in an emergency.

6. Instead of, "Wouldn't you like to find something to do?" you may find it more effective to say, "The book about Stevie that you liked so well last Sunday is on the bookrack; perhaps you would like to look at it again."

7. Instead of, "Let me show you how to make a bird's nest out of the clay," use, "You may make whatever you wish from the clay." If the child has asked how to make a bird's nest, say, "We have a real one in the cabinet. I'll get it so that you can look at it."

8. Instead of, "I'll cut out the hard part for you," say,

[1] Read, *The Nursery School* (Philadelphia: W. B. Saunders Co., 1955), p. 61. Used by permission of author and publisher.

"I'll draw a black line with the crayon, and you can cut along that line. It's pretty hard to cut those little places, isn't it?" (Seek to steer the child away from attempting something beyond his skill.)

9. Instead of, "I told you once to pick up the paper," say, "Here is the waste basket to put the pieces in when you pick them up," and then, if an additional suggestion is needed, "Do you want me to help you, or would you rather pick it up by yourself?"

10. Anticipate trouble and give a suggestion before it arises. Getting to the scene before one child hits another is better than afterwards.

11. Such rules as, "We keep our feet out of the chairs," should be very clear to each child and should apply each time the child is in his room. Every organization should have the same general rules for the age group.

12. Although teachers should usually not be a part of a group, they should be in a position where they can see what is going on in various areas. Rarely, if ever, should two teachers be together during activity time.

13. Watch for and eliminate situations in which a child is likely to be hurt.

14. Don't talk to another worker after a child is in the room on Sunday morning! Observe everything the children do and write down incidents that seem significant. If a child is having problems, it may be well to write down everything he does during a period of several weeks. This record will help in understanding and interpreting his behavior.

II. In the Use of Materials

In a training class, teachers' meeting, or some other time (other than Sunday morning) workers should use all of the materials in the department in the same way that the children will use them. In this way workers will become familiar with the materials and recognize problems which the child may meet in their use.

Children will need to be told over and over that "we do it this way." Workers who are tempted to become impatient must remind themselves how many times God forgives us when we break his commandments. We must be ready to forgive "seventy times seven" times if necessary.

The following suggestions are often used in the routine use of materials:

1. *Blocks*

Blocks are used in front of the shelf, on the floor.

They are to be returned to the shelf when the child is through with them.

They should be stacked neatly, with those of the same size together.

2. *Books*

Books are to be used in front of the bookrack unless there is some reason for using them in some other area. In some instances, one may be taken to some other part of the room to be used as a reference or part of an activity.

Children are to turn the pages of the book carefully, one at a time, so the pages will not be torn.

Hands must be clean when handling books.

3. *Nature Materials*

Nature materials should be handled very carefully, since many of them are delicate. They should be returned to the shelf after examination.

When bringing water from the bathroom for plants, the child should walk slowly and carefully, holding his finger over the spout of the watering can.

Fish should be fed only under the direct supervision of the teacher.

4. *Clay*

Children always wear smocks (made from men's shirts worn backwards) when working with clay. Often plastic aprons are provided to be worn over the smocks.

Clay is to be used on clay boards (or on the designated table, if boards are not being used).

Children may pound on the clay as hard as they wish.

Unless some special project is planned, the clay is to be returned to the clay jar at cleanup time (or whenever the child has finished with it).

These principles apply only to hard clay. Play dough is often used in the home and is entirely different.

5. *Easel Painting.*

Children always wear smocks when painting.

Brushes are to be wiped on each side before they are removed from the paint jar.

Each brush is to be used only in the jar where it belongs and is to be returned to that jar after use.

Children wipe up any dripped or spilled paint with a wet sponge.

Children wash their hands before removing their smocks.

At cleanup time, lids are put on the paint jars, brushes are washed and stored with the bristles down.

6. *Puzzles*

The child takes the puzzle from the puzzle rack to the puzzle table or to the floor near the rack.

He takes the pieces out, one at a time, and places them to his left on the table.

If he cannot finish the puzzle, another child or a teacher may help him.

When the puzzle is finished, he puts it back on the puzzle rack (or on the shelf, if there is no puzzle rack).

7. *Crayons*

A child may take a box of crayons from the art shelf to the table when he wishes to use them. They will be shared with others at the table.

Teachers may remove the paper from crayons, so that the child may color with the side for unusual effects.

Crayons are to be used only on large (12 by 18 inch) sheets of paper.

8. *Scissors and Paste*

Scissors are to be used only when the child is seated at the table or on the floor.

Children are to pick up scraps of paper and put them in the wastepaper basket.

Paste is to be used only on the corners of the paper being pasted.

Teachers may place a small amount of paste on a jar lid or saucer and put it in the center of the table. The children may get the amount they need from that container with paste sticks or brushes. Wooden "popsicle" sticks or tongue depressors may be used for paste sticks. Inexpensive paste sticks are available from Baptist Book Stores or school supply houses.

A damp sponge or paper towel should be placed within the reach of each child, so that he can wipe paste from his hands, the table, or his picture.

9. *Homeliving Materials*

The homeliving materials are to be used in the home.

Play dough is used on the cabinet or table (never on the floor). The lid must be placed on the play dough container after each use.

Dress-up clothes are to be put away in the proper place before group time.

Dishes are to be arranged neatly on the shelf at cleanup time.

The doll may be dressed and undressed as the children desire. At cleanup time, she should be dressed and placed on the bed. Extra clothes should be put in the proper place.

10. *Recordings*

The record should be left in the envelope until it is put on the record player, and returned to the envelope as soon as it has been played. Records should be handled at the edges, keeping fingers off recordings.

The record should be placed on the player, the arm placed on the record, and the player turned on. When the record has been played and the player turned off, the arm should be lifted and then the record removed.

III. WHEN CHILDREN ARE NOT WORKING TOGETHER

"Be ye kind" is very difficult to teach. Take notes in your department some morning and write down the number of times a child is unkind to another.

Lest they become too critical, workers should think back over their own experiences for the past week. Are there not times when they could have been more kind?

What should be the teacher's reaction when a child is unkind to another? Certainly the child's individual needs, and his own feelings which made him react in an unkind manner, must be considered.

Danny and Johnny had worked for a long time on a very intricate block building. Sue became very angry because Janice would not play with her and, turning around, kicked the block building down. Both boys began to cry, and Sue was on the verge of tears when a teacher reached her.

"I'm very sorry. Perhaps you will have time to build it back before group time," the teacher told Danny and Johnny.

Taking Sue by the hand, she led her out of the room.

She said nothing about apologizing, because she knew that Sue was not really sorry. And she knew that Sue recognized that she had been naughty.

They sat on the front steps of the church—the only place available where they could be alone. The teacher sat quietly for a few moments while Sue cried. Then she said, "I know how you feel, Sue. You wanted Janice to play with you, and she didn't want to. Sometimes I am very angry when people don't want to do the things I want them to do. Everyone feels that way sometimes.

"You felt better after you kicked the blocks, didn't you? But how do you suppose Danny and Johnny felt? They had worked so hard on that building. You don't like for someone to tear your things down, do you?

"When some people are angry they like to pound on the clay. Some people like to paint until they feel better. You might try that sometime when you are angry. But you must try to remember not to do something that will make someone else unhappy just because you are angry.

"I believe you could find someone to play with you if you would like to try again. Lynn is looking at a book all by herself. You could sit by her and look at another book. Or you might go to the home and pretend you are a visitor who came to see the sick baby." Seeing that Sue was interested, the teacher went on, "You could knock on the door as soon as we get back in our room."

"But where is the door?" Sue asked.

"Can you find something for a playlike door?"

"I could knock on the table," Sue suggested.

They went back to the room and Sue entered into the play in the home, following the teacher's suggestion that she be a visitor.

The teacher had recognized that Sue's problem was a feeling of rejection. She had two older sisters who made life miserable for her by refusing to let her play with them and their friends. She was not even allowed to go into their room at home. Perhaps Sue's hostility was directed as much toward the sisters as towards Janice.

The teacher recognized how important it was for Sue to be accepted by a group. She remained within hearing distance of Sue for the remainder of the morning so that she would be available for help if it were needed.

The rolling pin was a favorite toy with one group of four-year-olds. Nancy was making cookies from play dough one morning when Bill joined her and asked to use the rolling pin. She said no, but when she laid it down to put her cookies in the oven, Bill grabbed it. Nancy tried to get it away from him and began to cry when she was unsuccessful.

"Nancy was using the rolling pin, Bill," the teacher said. "Do you want to put it back on the table where you found it or give it back to her?"

Bill thought for a minute and then put the rolling pin on the table near Nancy's dough. "Nancy, you may finish your cookies now," the teacher said. "Maybe you will want to share the rolling pin with Bill in a few minutes. He would like to make some cookies, too."

In working out these problems, give the child a choice whenever possible. He responds much better to, "You may let Jimmy have one of the cars, and you may keep one. You decide which one you want to keep," than to, "Give Jimmy one of the cars."

Try never to embarrass a child. Take him out of the room if you need to talk with him more than just a moment. Remember that reasoning or talking in any form has little effect on the child who is emotionally disturbed. Wait until he becomes calm. "When you are through crying, you may tell me about it. I can understand what you are saying better if you aren't crying."

IV. WHEN A CHILD IS NOT TAKING PART IN ANY ACTIVITY

When Johnny sits and does not participate on Sunday morning, teachers may say: "Isn't Johnny good this morning? He is so quiet, and he isn't bothering anyone."

Actually, teachers should be more concerned about the child who is sitting alone and doing nothing than about the one who is entirely too noisy as he works.

We should ask ourselves some questions when we see Johnny sitting alone. First, are there several interesting things he could be doing? Have materials been varied from week to week so that he has not become bored? Second, is he a new child? If he has not attended Sunday school before, or if he is new in this particular department, sitting alone may be considered normal. He does not feel secure in his new surroundings, and we should not push him into an activity until he is ready.

David was such a child. Although he was four years old, he had never been to Sunday school. The first day he seemed very happy until his mother left. Then he stood by the door crying softly until she returned. He was so insistent upon staying by the door on the following Sundays that the teachers placed a chair there for him. Home visits failed to win his confidence, although he stopped crying on Sunday.

One morning there were two chairs near the door. On one was a book about one of David's favorite subjects— dogs. When no one was looking, he picked up the book and seemed to be enjoying it thoroughly until a teacher approached him to talk about it. He closed the book and refused to talk.

The workers recognized that David would come into the group of his own accord when he was ready. Each Sunday they greeted him warmly but did not insist on his participating. In just a few weeks he joined a nearby group.

Often a mother needs to remain with a new child until he feels secure in the room. Mother should never leave without telling him she is going, or he may really be frightened. Mother's purse, the car keys, or Daddy's hat left in the room will often assure the child that his parents will return.

If a child receives a home visit before he attends Sunday school, workers may suggest that his mother bring him to the church to see his room before Sunday. With only his mother and a teacher he has met before present, he will feel free to explore and get acquainted with the materials. On the following Sunday, he will find that meeting a large number of strange children can't be so bad when he already feels that he is in "his own" room.

If the child is not new in the department, workers should ask themselves another question: "Is his lack of participation habitual?" If the answer to this question is no, then we should consider first his health.

"Does he feel well this morning?" It will probably not be good to ask him, but a teacher might touch his head to see if he has fever, without letting him know what she is doing. On some occasions she might ask to see his throat. Parents usually appreciate knowing when their child has not acted as if he felt well, and the worker should give such information to them (not in the presence of the child) when they call for him.

One Sunday a teacher noticed that a child was not participating. Continued observation made her suspect that he was not well, and she shared this information with the parents when they came for him.

Although the mother had seen no evidence of his being ill, she took him home instead of remaining for the worship service. Later that afternoon she called to tell the teacher that he was breaking out with measles!

When a child is not feeling well, it is always wise to remove him from the group if possible. Every care should be taken to prevent exposing other children to contagion.

If the child who is not participating is feeling well physically, perhaps something has happened at home or on the way to church to cause him to want to be alone. Respect his privacy and give him time to sit and think, if that is what he needs. Listen if he wants to talk.

For the child who habitually sits without participating, perhaps home contacts are the most helpful way of bringing him out of his shell. Never talk about his lack of participation in his presence.

A teacher may take such a child with her when she goes to the woods to collect nature materials or for some other weekday activity. He might be asked to help clean the cabinet or some other project in the room, giving him an hour or two alone with a teacher. After one or two such experiences, ask him to choose another child to participate in another weekday activity with a teacher. Gradually he may feel more secure and may want to participate.

We must remember, however, that children are not all alike and that we cannot fit them into the same pattern. We will respect the right of Jimmy to be quiet if that is his nature. A casual invitation for him to join in some activity may be worthwhile, but begging or insisting usually will not help the shy child and may actually be harmful.

"It is all right for you to sit over here if you don't want to work with any of the children this morning. Would you like to look at this book while you sit here?"

V. WHEN AN UNDESIRABLE ACTIVITY HAS BEEN INITIATED

There is a difference in not wishing to participate in any activity because of shyness and in wanting to run around the room or play cowboy and Indian instead of working with another group.

Sherrie was a very immature four-year-old. She came into the room one morning and invited her friend, Sue, to "play chase" with her. Immediately Sherrie chased Sue around the room. A teacher stopped them on the first trip around and explained that they could build with blocks or paint or work puzzles or play in the home, but they could not run inside. Sue went back to the activity she had started before Sherrie came, and Sherrie wandered toward another area of the room.

Within five minutes, Sherrie was chasing Sue around the room again. The same teacher stopped them and patiently explained again that they could not run inside. She described some of the activities in which other children were participating and suggested that they join one group. This time she stayed with them until each one was seemingly settled in some worthwhile activity.

The activity did not last, however, and a few minutes later Sherrie had induced Sue to join her in another game of "chase." Since Sherrie was definitely the leader, the teacher sent Sue back to her activity, and took Sherrie aside. "Sherrie, you may not run in Sunday school," she said firmly. "I know you like to 'play chase' with Sue, but you must wait until sometime when you can play outside. Today you may work puzzles or help build the hospital with blocks or play house. You may decide which you want to do."

"I don't want to do anything but play chase. If I can't play chase, I won't do anything!" Sherrie pouted.

"It is all right with me if you don't want to do anything, Sherrie. You may sit right here in this chair until the others are through working. Then we will bring our chairs over here for group time."

Sherrie was amazed. The teacher knew enough about her home background to realize that this was one of the few times in her life when Sherrie had failed to get her way by pouting. She remained in her chair for the remainder of the session, however, and that was the last of "playing chase."

Children need some emphatic no's. They are much more secure when they recognize that teachers will say no when it is necessary, and that begging or tears or threats will not change the no to yes.

Danny went through a stage of refusing to participate in any activity. He roamed from one section of the room to another and disturbed every group. The workers were frantic.

On her first day in the department a new worker was given the responsibility of "handling Danny." Sensing that there had been little firmness in the past, she explained to him that he could choose what he wanted to do, but that he must do one of those things or else sit down and wait for group time. He could not roam around and disturb others.

Danny argued, but the teacher was firm. "I don't like to do any of those things," Danny kept insisting.

"Then you don't have to do them. You may just sit over here until group time."

Eventually Danny reluctantly joined a group in block building and seemed to enjoy participating.

The teacher wondered what their relationship would be in the future. Would he hate her for being too strict? Had she been as kind to him as she had wanted to be? She remembered, "Be gentle unto all," and hoped that she had been gentle in her dealings with Danny. "Friendly firmness" had been her goal, but had she reached it?

After church, she met Danny's mother in the corridor. Danny was not with her. "What in the world did you do to Danny today?" she asked. "You really made a friend. He cried because I wouldn't let him sit with you in church!"

Teachers will have different ideas about what is desirable and what is undesirable in the use of the various materials. Some feel that any play activity must be centered around a church or something related to a church. Others feel that the child should play out his own experiences and the teachers should interpret and use these experiences as best they can. Each group of workers must determine what their policy will be and select materials which will stimulate interest along desired lines.

Some workers feel that a child should never be allowed to play war games or cowboy games. Others feel that letting the child initiate his own activities is best, and if he continually builds corrals or forts to protect the settlers from the Indians, the teachers should be concerned not about his Sunday activity, but about his seeing too many television programs that stimulate such activity. A parent meeting to discuss the selection of children's programs may be the solution.

If teachers feel that some type of activity should not be allowed, group time may be the place to discuss the problem. Talk with the children about the kind of things they may build and the things they are not to build or play. Give them satisfying reasons.

Children need more than one reminder, just as adults must be reminded again and again of the things God would have them do.

FOR CLASS DISCUSSION

Decide on a better way to word the following:

"Don't stand in the chair."
"Come back and pick up your blocks."
"You can't play with the doll now."
"Don't write on the walls with the crayon."
"Don't take the dishes to the puzzle table."
"Our Bible verse is 'We are helpers.' Can you say it?"
"Would you like to go to group time now?"
"You were bad to hit Judy."

FOR FURTHER STUDY

Read, Katherine H. *The Nursery School.*

CHAPTER 8

8

Teaching in Group Time

THE last part of the morning session with Beginners is called group time. The length varies with the age of the children. Most Three-Year-Nursery departments have a group time of twelve to fifteen minutes, so children coming from a Nursery department in October should not be expected to participate in a longer group time for the first month. Gradually it may be increased during the year.

Children usually sit in a semicircle during group time, with the superintendent in the front. Workers sit in the circle rather than behind it. If there are children who are likely to cause disturbance, the workers may tactfully sit near them without the children's being conscious of their motive.

I. TEACHING THROUGH BIBLE VERSES

Many years ago Beginners were taught a "memory verse" each Sunday. In today's departments for four's and five's there is no designated memory verse, but selected Bible verses are used every Sunday. As the child hears them used over and over, he is not only learning to repeat them; he is using the verse in experiences which enrich its meaning and relate it to conduct.

1. *Planned Use of Verses*

The superintendent should have the children use several Bible verses in group time. Suggestions are usually given in the teacher's quarterly and may include such activities as finding marked verses in the Bible and "reading" them together, matching verses with pictures, or singing verses which have been set to music.

2. *Incidental Use of Verses*

In addition to verses selected as the session is planned, the alert superintendent will use many others incidentally. She should know all of the verses familiar to the children and be able to locate them quickly in her Bible.

If Bing comments on Sunday morning that Grandmother is coming to see him next week, the superintendent may answer, "I'm so glad God planned for children to have grandmothers. I read in my Bible, 'God is good.'"

When Pam calls attention to the flowers she arranged, the superintendent may read, "God . . . hath made every thing beautiful" (Eccl. 3:10–11). Teachers should always read the verse from the Bible, so that the child will associate the verse with the Bible. Children may be encouraged to recall verses as the occasion arises.

II. TEACHING THROUGH THE BIBLE STORY

Each Sunday's lesson materials include a Bible story, selected because of its teaching values for four's and five's, in the light of the age-group objectives and the unit purpose.

When the Bible stories selected for one year's lessons were compared with the age-group objectives as listed in chapter 3, workers discovered that each story is directly related to one or more of the teaching objectives and each objective is covered by one or more stories.

1. *Emphasizing Its Importance*

One of the most important elements of group time is the Bible story. The superintendent should study it thoroughly and master it so that there is no need to refer to notes or to the book. In fact, only in rare instances should the teacher's book be brought to Sunday school.

"What Bible story did you hear this morning?" a mother asked her Beginner.

"We didn't have one today," was his reply.

"But you always have a Bible story," Mother answered. "Did you have any story today?"

"We had a story about Philip telling the man in the chariot about Jesus."

"But that's a Bible story," Mother interrupted.

"She didn't tell it out of the Bible; she told it out of a magazine," was his honest reply.

The storyteller should always sit with the open Bible in her lap as she tells the story. "I read that story right here in my Bible," she may say.

When the story for the day was completed, a superintendent remarked, "I know that is a true story because I read it in my Bible."

"You mean it really happened?" Walter asked in amazement.

When the superintendent assured him that all Bible stories really happened, Walter could hardly believe her. "I never knew that before," he said.

2. *Mastering Storytelling Technique*

In order not to detract from the story itself, the storyteller should not have any objects in her hand while telling it. She should not wear a hat nor dangling earrings or bracelets. She should avoid gestures. The attention of the children should be on what she is saying rather than on what she is doing with her hands.

"I like this story. I hope you will like it," should be her attitude. Avoid such negative suggestions as: "Now sit still so I can tell you the story." Such a request suggests to the child that the story won't be very interesting, but is something that he must endure with patience.

Pause, take a deep breath, and smile before you start the story. Relax. Pitch your voice low, talk distinctly and not too loud. Avoid hurrying. Forget yourself and focus your attention on the children and the story.

The lesson writer has spent hours in research and study as well as in the actual writing of the story. Certainly the story as it is printed should help you to make skilful use of words and concepts which are meaningful to the children. But you will usually hold their attention better if you do not attempt to memorize the story. Memorizing the first and last sentences may prove helpful.

If you have told the story often during the week, you will not forget it on Sunday. Practice telling the story every day. Many workers find that telling it in front of a mirror is helpful. Tell it as you wash dishes or make beds. Read the story from the Bible and from the quarterly every day. Write it in your own words. Most important of all, pray that God will help you to use the story to help the boys and girls.

III. Teaching Through the Use of Music

One of the teaching elements of group time is music. Each song used should be carefully selected, with the desired outcome, special needs and interests of the children, and the activity-time experiences considered. Although the superintendent may have a general idea of songs which may be used, there will be changes as the responses of the children are given consideration.

1. *Ways of Using Music*

The use of music with four's and five's is not limited to a particular portion of the group time procedure. It will be used purposefully in many ways.

(1) *To interpret an experience.*—For example, the conversation may be centered around church experiences and ways the children may help at church. The song "My Church" would contribute to this experience.

My Church

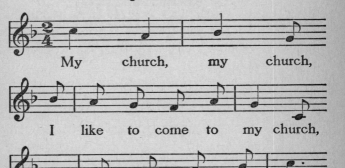

My church, my church,

I like to come to my church,

We learn of Je - sus here,

We learn of Je - sus here.

Words and music by Ruth Reed. From *Songs for 4's and 5's.*
© Copyright 1960, Broadman Press.

Suppose that, during the conversation about the church, a cardinal flies to the window sill and the children watch him eat from a feeding station they have prepared. The first stanza of "I Wonder" might be used, even though it had not been planned for that Sunday.

I Wonder

I won-der, I won-der,

I won-der a-bout the birds
I won-der a-bout the sun
I won-der a-bout the moon
I won-der a-bout the wind

That fly so high,
That shines so bright,
That shines at night,
That blows oo oo,

God sends the birds up in the sky.
God sends the sun to give us light.
God sends the moon with sil - v'ry light.
God sends the wind that blows oo - oo.

Words and music by John Clark. From *Songs for 4's and 5's*.
© Copyright 1960, Broadman Press.

Sometimes an experience related by a child may suggest a song to be sung by the entire group, or by a teacher. If Karen tells how she helped Mother and Daddy rake the leaves, the superintendent may sing "Our Home."

Our Home

1. Our home is such a hap-py place,
We're bus-y all the day;
There's so much work for us to do,
So man-y games to play.

2. Our home is such a hap-py place,
The nic-est place I know;
We work to-geth-er ev-'ry day
To help to make it so.

Words anonymous. Music by Jane Dorsey. From *Songs for 4's and 5's,* copyright 1960, Broadman Press.

Since the use of many songs cannot be anticipated, piano accompaniment is not necessary. If there is a piano, it is important that the pianist memorize all of the songs so that she can play them without the delay of finding the music. Some workers prefer the autoharp for accompaniment, especially in a very crowded room.

(2) *To create a mood.*—As some children complete noisy activities and come to the group, the superintendent may sing softly, "God Is Very Near," or the pianist may play a hymn tune.

God Is Very Near

God is ver-y near;

God is ver-y near;

He hears us when we sing and pray,

God is ver-y near.

Words by Aurora M. Shumate. Music by Hazel Watlington. From *Songs We Sing*, copyright 1939, Broadman Press.

She may find that the song helps the children to become quiet and reverent. (Care should be taken that any such use of songs does not become routine, however, or it will lose its effectiveness.) The use of "Happy Sunday Morning" or "I Like to Go to Church" may create a happy mood, while "I Love Jesus" or "I Wonder" may be used when feelings of awe or reverence are desired.

Instrumental recordings also have a place in creating a mood.

(3) *To motivate conduct.*—Music may be used to motivate a pattern of conduct. "Love One Another," "I Will Be a

Helper," or "Thank You, God, for Prayertime" (all from *Songs for 4's and 5's,* Broadman Press) may be used in this way. Singing "Thank You, God, for Prayertime" *may* encourage some Beginner to ask his parents to initiate a prayertime at his house. Singing "Share with One Another" (one stanza of "Love One Another") *may* encourage him to be more generous with his toys.

(4) *For strengthening teaching.*—Music may be used for teaching a truth. Although memorization does not guarantee learning in any sense, there is value in teaching Bible truths and verses through songs if the child is given experiences to help him interpret them. "God Made Everything Beautiful," if used with autumn leaves, spring flowers, or with pictures of beautiful things God made, will help the child's concept of God's creative work to grow. "We . . . are helpers" (2 Cor. 1:24) will take on new meaning to the child if used with "I Will Be a Helper" and related through conversation and pictures to ways the child can help.

(5) *For relaxation.*—For the four- or five-year-old relaxation through activity is essential to learning. Children will

God Made Everything Beautiful

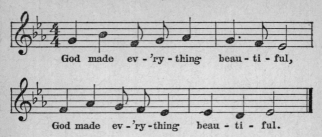

Ecclesiastes 3:11. Music by Jane Dorsey. From *Songs for 4's and 5's,* copyright 1960, Broadman Press.

enjoy "being" Downy Duck or the bunny as they sing "Quack, Quack, Quack" or "Our Bunny's So Funny." "Tell Us What You See" or "I'm Very, Very Tall" give opportunities for relaxing muscles that have become tired from too much sitting.

2. *Some Guiding Principles*

Use a song instead of *teaching* a song. Avoid repeating words as drill.

To help the child understand and appreciate the words, many workers sing the song first with only the melody played on the piano. After the children have learned the song, full accompaniment may be added.

Avoid use of motions with worship songs. Motion songs should be used only rarely, and then for relaxation.

Select songs with words which express feelings or emotions which the child himself may have. There is little value for the average Beginner in singing "Thank You, Lord, for Saving My Soul," but he can sincerely sing:

> We thank You, now dear God,
> For all the things You give us.
> From *Songs for 4's and 5's*

Select songs with simple melodies, with music suitable for the words. The average range of young children's voices is from D to D.

It is important that the child learn good music during the time that his appreciation of music is being formed.

IV. TEACHING THROUGH CONVERSATION

The group time should include informal, but guided, conversation between the children and workers. There should be a sharing of experiences and discussion of problems by the entire group.

1. *Introducing Conversation*

As the occasion arises, the following, or similar, introductions to conversation might be used:

"There were many helpers in our room while you were working this morning. Would you like to tell us about someone who helped you?"

"In church this morning Mrs. Lee will play pretty music on the organ. I am going to sit very quietly and listen to the music. Tell me something else I will hear in church."

"I brought some money to Sunday school this morning. Some of it will be used to buy the pictures we use in our room every week. Can you think of something else the money will be used for?"

"When we were getting ready for group time this morning, Ken was carrying a chair and bumped into Susan and pushed her down. Ken did not want to hurt Susan, and he is very sorry. Can you help Ken to think of a way he can carry his chair so that he will not bump into someone else?"

"Some of us pushed our chairs across the room this morning, and they made a noise. Do you think the people in the next room were bothered by our noise? How can we get our chairs over here for group time without pushing them?"

2. *Some Principles to Follow*

Conversation should not go on and on until the children become bored and restless. The superintendent must be alert to the children's needs at all times. During informal conversation, she may wish to follow the principle of not telling the children anything that she can get them to tell her.

Workers, as well as children, must remember that only one person talks at a time, or no one can be heard. Avoid interrupting a child unless absolutely necessary. In large groups it may be necessary for each child to raise his hand and secure permission to speak, but a more informal procedure is desirable.

In addition to conversations initiated by the workers, children frequently have experiences they want to relate. Whether the child will be given time for sharing will be determined by the child's needs, the attention span of the group, and other factors.

Lynn, who had never participated in any conversation during activity time or group time, was given all the time he wanted when he finally "opened up" and wanted to tell the group about their new garage door. On the same Sunday, Walter, who wanted to talk all the time every Sunday, was reminded that there was not time for him to tell the group about his trip to the lake, but perhaps he could tell some of the other children about it while they worked together next Sunday.

Whether the teacher comments on the child's contributions to the conversation will be determined by the individual child's needs and the teaching value of such comments. When Alice told the group that her mother and daddy had a big fight before Sunday school, the superintendent went on to something else without comment. When Kerry showed his new shoes, however, the group discussed how Kerry was growing so much that he couldn't wear his old shoes any more, and thanked God for helping children grow.

In the conversation, avoid anything that would embarrass a child. Be as tactful with children as you would be with adults.

V. TEACHING THROUGH PICTURES

Pictures are one of the means by which spiritual truths are interpreted to children. The wise use of pictures in group time requires careful planning.

1. *Sources of Pictures*

In addition to the teaching picture for the day, other pictures should be used each Sunday. Every department should have a file for Beginner teaching pictures and carefully selected and mounted pictures from other sources, such as magazines, and calendars. *Teaching Pictures for Four's and Five's* are published for use in Sunday school and Training Union departments. Workers will want to make them available for use in Sunbeam Band, music activity, Vacation Bible school, study courses, and other Beginner activities.

2. *Ways of Using Pictures*

A just-from-the-Nursery group of four-year-olds had as the theme for the day "Happy Times Singing at Church." As a picture activity during group time, three children were selected (one at a time) to walk around the room and find a picture of someone who was singing. The verse, "Sing praises" (Psalm 9:11) was read after each picture was found. Then another child was chosen to find a picture of something else that sings (a robin). The pictures used showed children singing at Sunday school, a family joining in the congregational singing in a worship service, and a robin.

As the children grow and have more experiences in the

department, their picture activities will vary. The superintendent may read a verse and then ask a child to find a picture which reminds him of that verse. Five-year-olds may look at a series of pictures and place them in correct sequence. For example, after the story of the good Samaritan has been told, the superintendent may display the following pictures (which will be found in the files if pictures have been kept over a period of several years) and ask the children to arrange them in order:

The Samaritan paying the innkeeper as they stand by the bed of the sick man;

The Samaritan pouring oil on the wounds;

The Samaritan and the hurt man (on the donkey) at the door of the inn;

The Samaritan lifting the hurt man to put him on the donkey.

3. *Interpretation of Pictures*

Frequently children may point out that the people do not look alike in various pictures representing the same story. For example, each of the four pictures of the good Samaritan shows a different man as the Samaritan and a different man as the hurt man.

If the children are not conscious of this difference, the workers will want to call it to their attention. "These aren't real pictures of Bible people. We don't know how they really looked. A man named _____ painted this picture. He read the story in the Bible, and he painted the picture the way he thought the people looked. Another man named _____ painted this picture the way he thought the people looked. (The artist's name is usually in the lower right-hand corner of the picture.)

"When two of you paint pictures of houses or trees or flowers, your pictures do not look alike. God made us so that we do things differently. If you like, some day you may paint a picture of the good Samaritan the way you think he looked." Be very sure that the children understand that we have no real pictures of Jesus—only pictures of how people think he looked.

The picture illustrating any story is usually not used until after the story has been told. The exception to this principle is the picture which is essential to the understanding of some detail in the story. For example, a picture of a flat-roofed house shown before the story will eliminate misunderstanding as children hear about the room for Elisha or the man let down through the roof.

VI. Teaching Through Relaxation

God did not make four- and five-year-olds to be still. Growing muscles demand action, and relaxation is essential during group time. Its use helps to keep children alert and responsive to spiritual experiences. Teachers must direct, rather than suppress, the child's activity. The teacher who insists that the children remain still can be assured that the children will develop a dislike for her and for the situation, and that her efforts to teach Bible truths will thus be robbed of their effectiveness.

Many of the elements of group time also provide relaxation. Picture activities, where a child (or in small departments, the entire group of children) walks around the room to look for pictures, provide excellent relaxation. Often the child who is becoming restless will be the one selected to choose a ribbon from the Bible or to bring a book from the bookrack.

Usually the purpose for the day can be considered in the selection of relaxation activities. When the creation story is being used, the record "Let's Sing About Creation" may be played and the children encouraged to "be" the animals as they are described. This record describes the creation, then in another part, the animals. Thus, the action is not a part of the worship theme of the record. When the emphasis is on growing things, the children may play out planting, hoeing, watering, and harvesting fruits or vegetables to the tune of "Mulberry Bush." When the story of Ruth or baby Moses has been told, the children may play it out.

Games, such as "Rocking," are often used for relaxation, and may be useful also in helping children learn to take turns and to learn one another's names. Frequently this game (or others of a similar nature) may be used during the time when children are waiting for parents at the end of the Sunday school session.

Rocking

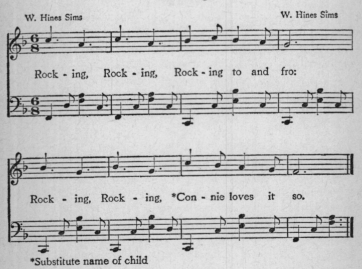

W. Hines Sims — W. Hines Sims

Rock - ing, Rock - ing, Rock - ing to and fro:

Rock - ing, Rock - ing, *Con - nie loves it so.

*Substitute name of child

© Copyright 1960, Broadman Press.

There should be a continuity of each of the elements of group time, with each tying into the next. Nothing should be used without a definite reason. Careful planning as well as an alert attitude toward the interests and needs of the children are essential.

FOR CLASS DISCUSSION

Using the purpose, "To help each child grow in his appreciation of his home and his parents and to grow in his willingness to help at home," make plans for a group time procedure. Include in your plans each of the elements mentioned in this chapter.

FOR FURTHER STUDY

Dillard, Polly Hargis. *The Church Kindergarten*. Chap. 6.

Read, Katherine H. *The Nursery School*. Chap. 10.

Shields, Elizabeth McE. *Music in the Religious Growth of Children*. Nashville: Abingdon Press, 1943.

Thomas, Edith Lovell. *Music in Christian Education*. Nashville: Abingdon Press, 1943.

CHAPTER 9

9

Parents as Fellow Teachers

SUNDAY school workers have the children from one hour to an hour and a half each week. Some Beginners are in kindergarten or nursery school ten to fifteen hours a week. For the remainder of the time, most of them are with their parents. Whether they realize it or not, parents are doing more teaching than any other person in the child's life.

The story is told of a number of baby sharks and baby crabs that played together on the bottom of the ocean. They had delightful times, but the crabs had a habit which annoyed the sharks greatly—they always swam backwards.

The sharks resolved to teach their friends to swim properly. Early one morning they began the lessons and by evening the crabs were swimming forward.

The next morning the sharks eagerly awaited the arrival of their friends. When they saw the crabs swimming backward to the playground, the sharks were greatly annoyed. The entire day was spent in teaching the crabs to swim forward.

The same thing happened for several days. Finally, in desperation, the sharks resolved to go home with the crabs to try to find out why they forgot how to swim forward overnight.

When they reached the crabs' home, they discovered why their teaching was ineffective. The mother and father crabs came out to meet them—swimming backward.

Unless parents and teachers are working together, many of the goals of religious education will never be reached.

I. WORKING WITH PARENTS MEANS SHARING GOALS

Susy is encouraged to be a helper, and ways for helping are suggested in Sunday school. Susy may be challenged to hang up her own pajamas and to help set the table. If Mother does not understand that Susy is learning, "We . . . are helpers," however, she may not be willing to take the extra time required to let Susy "help." Parents should know the aim for each unit of work. They should know verses, songs, and stories which may be used in the home.

Teachers may be leading children to pray in their own words, while parents who do not know of this goal may be leading the child to *say* a prayer instead of talking to God.

Parents often do not understand the goals in art activities and place too much emphasis on the finished product. One mother expected her child, who had just begun painting, to identify each object in her paintings.

"What's that?" she asked when Martha greeted her at the door and eagerly displayed a painting.

"Can't you see? It's a picture," Martha answered.

Mother, still not recognizing that the child had painted *ideas* instead of *things*, pointed to a big blob of red paint on the corner of the paper. "What's that?" she asked.

"Mother, you ought to be able to see that's red paint!" she answered in disgust.

Teachers had not helped parents to understand the purpose of painting, so this mother was undoing some of the things the teachers were attempting to do.

Sharing goals with parents should not be one-way communication. They, too, sometimes more than the teachers, see the child's needs and have goals for his development.

One group of parents was asked to write notes to the workers stating one thing they would especially like for the teachers to do for their child during the year. Such things as teaching him to pray, helping to overcome shyness, or helping him to appreciate Bible stories were mentioned. During the year, parents and teachers compared notes on the progress in these areas. Each received helpful suggestions from the others.

Some departments prepare a mimeographed sheet each month, giving the unit theme, desired outcomes, some of the activities which may be used, and some of the ways the teaching may be carried over into the home. These sheets may be shared with parents in visitation or may be mailed.

Some departments use a questionnaire at the beginning or the end of a unit to determine needs or to test teaching which has been done. A questionnaire similar to the following might be used preceding a unit on God's love and care. It would help to make parents aware of things to note.

---

1. Does your child often suggest thanking God for anything which has made him happy?
2. What experiences has he had which would help him understand how God provides the following:
    Food (for example, planting a garden)
    Clothing (for example, visiting a cotton or woolen mill, sheep ranch, or cotton field)
    Homes (visiting a sawmill or brick kiln)
3. Has he related any of these experiences to God?
4. Is thanks offered at mealtime in your home?
    By parent_____   Memorized prayer_____
    By child_____   Prayer in own words_____ .
5. Do you have any suggestions as to ways we can make the November emphasis, "Thanking God for His Love and Care," mean more to your child?

Parents help teachers in testing teaching. They know when the child applies the teaching to his life. They often know when Bible stories, verses, or songs are misunderstood, and they should be encouraged to share such information with the teachers.

II. WORKING WITH PARENTS MEANS SHARING KNOWLEDGE OF TEACHING METHODS

Teachers may be concerned about Melinda's lack of participation and may be doing everything possible to bring her out. On the other hand, Mother, who does not understand the procedure in today's Sunday school, may be insisting that Melinda "sit still and be quiet and be a good girl."

Most parents are interested in ways their children are taught.

"But when do you teach them? They seem to be playing all the time?"

"Shouldn't we teach Beginners a memory verse?"

"How do I know what his lesson is?"

"It doesn't make any difference if he is late, does it? Don't you just let them play for most of the time and then have Sunday school right at the last?"

The foregoing questions came from a parent meeting. They show how little parents actually knew about the procedure with four's and five's. The fault was not theirs.

Since many of these parents were teachers in other departments and could not observe in the Beginner room, another method of sharing was arranged.

The superintendent explained the purpose for a preceding Sunday, which happened to be "to help each child to know that God created animals and to appreciate God's gifts of animals." She explained and showed some of the materials which were selected for use on that day. The wooden animals were used on the block shelf, a stuffed dog and a dog food can in the home, books about animals on the bookrack, and a turtle, a jar of crayfish, and an ant colony on the nature shelf. She showed the pictures of various animals that had been placed in various parts of the room.

One by one the teachers told of experiences which they had observed in the use of these materials the previous

Sunday. They described problems which arose (not telling the children's names) and told how they were solved. The superintendent then shared some of the experiences from group time. Copies of songs used were thrown on the screen and the parents joined in singing them.

Parents were enthusiastic in their appreciation. Most of them indicated that this was the first attempt that had been made to explain to them how their children were taught.

III. Working with Parents Means Sharing Problems

"Danny won't listen to Bible stories any more," his mother told one of the teachers. "Can you give me any suggestions?"

"What should we do when Jane refuses to say her prayers?"

"Cherry's grandmother is critically ill, and will probably not live. How can we prepare Cherry for this experience of death?"

Such questions come from parents who have confidence in the ability of their child's Sunday school teacher. Teachers must guard against a "know it all" attitude, but should endeavor to help parents find an answer to their problems.

One of the best answers is, "I have a book that throws some light on that subject. Would you like to borrow it? I'll bring it to you." When the worker does not have such a book of her own, she may refer the parent to a book in the church or public library. If the parent is not a church member and is not familiar with the church library, the teacher may wish to arrange to meet her there or to take her to the library to find needed help.

Each teacher should have a supply of tracts, free leaflets, magazine and newspaper articles relating to common childhood problems. These may be made available for parents.

Often teachers may go to parents for help with special problems. Care must be taken in approaching the parent about behavior problems. Parents should understand that the teacher does not want them to attempt to force the child to conform in whatever problem he faces. Instead of, "We can't make Johnny behave, and we want you to try to do it," teachers should use the approach, "Johnny has a problem that we don't quite understand, and we wonder if you could help us." Often parents may not realize that behavior problems do have a cause, and workers must be very tactful in every approach.

In addition to behavior problems, there may be other needs. Parents may help in securing additional materials or equipment for the department or in sharing information of a specialized nature. The father who teaches biology may be able to give a great deal of help with the nature unit. The parents who spent a year abroad in military service may help with missionary units. Some mothers may make doll clothes, while some fathers may make equipment. Most parents are glad to share in the work of their child's department if they are made to feel that their help is wanted and needed. Sometimes even unsaved or unaffiliated parents may be enlisted in such projects, and this may be a way of interesting them in the program of the church.

IV. WORKING WITH PARENTS MEANS ENCOURAGING USE OF HOME PERIODICALS

Most Beginner departments provide Beginner pupils' books for home use, and many also provide *Home Life*. Both are valuable assets to religious education in the home if they are used properly.

Parents need to understand that the pupil's book is not lessons to be taught to the child but stories to be enjoyed. Some suggestions for its use in the home are included from time to time, and these should be pointed out to parents.

Take *Home Life* into the home instead of sending it, if at all possible. Giving literature to the parent on Sunday morning does not guarantee that it will reach the home; frequently it is left in the auditorium during the worship service.

If *Home Life* is distributed on Sunday morning, there is no opportunity to explain its use and to point out special articles relating to needs or interests of the parent. Many parents will not understand the use of "The Family Worships" and "The Family Teaches" (sections of *Home Life*) unless a teacher helps them to find and interpret these sections.

Encouraging parents to establish and maintain family worship may be the most helpful thing teachers can do for a child during the Beginner years. *Home Life* provides one of the best approaches for achieving this goal.

Parents will work with teachers if they understand what is expected of them. Through your visitation program, and your parent meetings, keep parents informed of your goals, your program, and your needs. Many of your objectives coincide with theirs. Together you may achieve the desired results.

FOR CLASS DISCUSSION

Compose a letter to parents explaining the aims, activities, and related home activities for one of the units in the current issue of the *Beginner Teacher*.

FOR FURTHER STUDY

Dillard, Polly Hargis. *The Church Kindergarten.* Chap. 10.
Heinz, Mamie W. *Growing and Learning in the Kindergarten.* Chap. 3.
Lambert, Hazel M. *Teaching the Kindergarten Child.* New York: Harcourt, Brace and Co., 1958. Chap. 17.
Read, Katherine H. *The Nursery School.* Chap. 13.

CHAPTER 10

10

The Challenge of Teaching Beginners

PAUL'S WORDS to Timothy, "Take heed unto thyself, and unto the doctrine," are an appropriate message to teachers.

I. THE CHALLENGE TO BE ATTRACTIVE

Beginner children like their workers to be attractive. One child, when being promoted to the Primary department, remarked, "I hope we have good-looking teachers this year."

Everyone cannot be a beauty, but everyone can look her best. A thoughtful writer puts the matter thus.

Does it make a difference in a woman's appearance whether or not her personality is Christ-controlled? Yes. And He is not an eccentric. He wants us to look our best. I believe we are responsible for what our faces and our bodies *say* to those whom we meet. . . .

A woman's grooming, her adornment, her size are definite indications of who is at the controls of her life.

Is Jesus Christ at the controls of your life?

. . . .

When a woman's twisted personality is straightened out, so will be the seams in her stockings and the part in her hair! He [Jesus] is interested in the total personality and this certainly includes our looks as well as our insight.

. . . .

Genuine good taste has to stem from God! After all, He is the one who had the infinite good taste to create crocuses, rainbows, small orchids and green ocean waves at sunset. All real beauty is His. And He will guide you. He knows where He placed you and with whom.[1]

[1] Eugenia Price, *Woman to Woman* (Grand Rapids: Zondervan Publishing House, 1959), pp. 91, 77, 84-85.

This reference was written for women. More and more men are now working in Beginner departments, and neatness and cleanliness are just as important for them as for women.

Not only should we be our best for the sake of the children, but for the sake of parents, who sometimes form their opinion of the church and of Christians by a Sunday school teacher.

But most important of all, the teacher should look her best for her own self-respect and in order that she might be a better witness for Christ.

II. THE CHALLENGE TO DEPENDABILITY AND CO-OPERATION

Karen, who had always loved Sunday school, announced one Sunday morning that she was not going. Because she was so positive about it, her mother recognized that this was not a sudden whim. Whether they would go was not a decision left for the children in this family, but the mother was concerned that Karen was not willing to go happily.

"Tell me why you don't want to go," Karen's mother said.

"Because Miss Virginia doesn't go any more," was Karen's reply. "If she stays home, I want to stay home, too."

Mother assured Karen that they would find out why Miss Virginia was not attending, and Karen agreed to go to Sunday school with the other members of the family.

In the Beginner room another teacher explained that Miss Virginia had been away for three weeks because of serious illness in her family. No one had thought to explain her absence to the children. Perhaps others, like Karen, had assumed that Miss Virginia did not want to come to Sunday school any more.

Often teachers who must be away write post cards to the department, explaining their absence. The cards can be shared at group time. A picture post card of the church the worker attended during her absence will assure the children that the worker is in Sunday school, even if she is not in their department.

Sometimes teachers teach more by the things they do not do than by the things they do. If Mrs. Jones talks with the children about the joy of going to the worship service to hear the pastor, and yet the children see her leave when Sunday school is over, she is teaching them that church is not very important. The teacher who is late without reason every Sunday cannot teach the children that Sunday school is important to her, regardless of what she may say.

Teaching the children to co-operate is one of the goals of Beginner work. Can the teacher who is not taking part in the church program of training or visitation or teachers' meeting teach co-operation to children? Of course, Beginners are not likely to know whether the teacher does these things, but co-operation is an attitude, and attitudes are caught more than they are taught. We teach a great deal more by what we are than by what we say.

Our co-operation and dependability reflect our concept of the importance of our task. If we believe Sunday school is important for Beginners, we will give our best to our task. The religious education of Beginners is important enough to deserve our best.

III. The Challenge to Consecration

Every Beginner worker should be in her place of service because of a deep conviction that this is the place God would have her be.

Beginner children deserve the best. Gone is the day when the belief that just anybody could "keep the children" was accepted. Four- and five-year-olds, like every other age group, deserve teachers who will spend time in prayer for every session, who will seek earnestly to win unsaved parents to Christ, and who are teaching because of a love for

Christ and a desire to share that love with their pupils. No other motive is worthy.

In a study course, a Beginner worker gave this story of her own experience. Her pastor and Sunday school superintendent visited in her home and asked her to give consideration to becoming Beginner superintendent the following year, and she refused. She had no interest in Beginners. A few days later they returned, saying they had prayed earnestly about the matter and felt deeply impressed that she was the one for the place. Again she refused.

The third time they came to visit they made this suggestion. "Would you pray earnestly for God to reveal to you the thing he wants you to do? We do not want you to take the place unless God wants you there. Are you willing to do whatever God wants you to do next year, regardless of what it is?"

She agreed to pray with them. Every day she asked God to reveal to her the place where he would have her serve. Within a week she had a deep conviction that she should accept the place as Beginner superintendent, trusting God to help her in the areas where she knew she was weakest. Her testimony was that during the years she had served in that position, she had never doubted that she was doing the thing God wanted her to do, and never once had the problems that she previously considered unsurmountable obstacles proved to be difficulties. God had provided the strength for her to do the thing he wanted her to do and had filled her life with deep satisfaction.

IV. THE CHALLENGE TO DEEPER STUDY

No age group in the Sunday school demands more study for effective work than does the Beginner. There are three areas in which every worker must study if she is to do her best.

1. *Of the Bible*

We must study not only the Bible stories we tell to the children, but the entire Bible for our own spiritual growth.

Every worker in the department should study her lesson every week. Curriculum materials give a background for the teacher's study in relation to the emphasis to be used each Sunday. Each teacher should read all of this background and all of the Bible references. Because children need repetition and stories are repeated frequently, teachers sometimes feel that there is no need for weekly study.

"I'm so sick of baby Moses I could die," a Beginner worker said as she came into the room one Wednesday evening. "Why do we have to study that story again tonight?"

The person who was leading the Bible study period of the teachers' meeting had given assignments for preparation. Each worker was to study the lesson prior to the meeting and to come prepared to share one practical application for her own life gained from the study. A portable chalkboard had been brought into the room (for Wednesday night only) and these practical applications were written on the board. As they were discussed, new ones were discovered. When the Bible study period was over, there were twelve lessons for each worker to use in her own spiritual growth. (These were not to be shared with the Beginners.)

"This was one of the most helpful lessons I've ever studied. I'll never complain about baby Moses again," said the teacher who had, at the beginning of the session, requested that they study "something new."

A thorough knowledge of the Bible is necessary for accurate interpretation of Bible stories. Teachers sometimes, without thinking, have their Old Testament characters quoting New Testament verses, or early New Testament characters quoting verses which were written in later New Testament times. David or Samuel could not have read, "Children, obey your parents," or, "Love one another," or, "Be gentle unto all."

Although we do not give all of many passages to the Beginner child because of his limited understanding, we want all that is given him to be correct. He should not have to "unlearn" what we have taught him as he grows older.

There are many helps for Bible study. A Bible dictionary and a one-volume Bible commentary are a good investment for any Bible student. There are many books which are useful in understanding and interpreting the Scriptures.

Each worker should have a Bible study plan, in addition to the study of each Sunday's lesson. Haphazard reading too often results in the rereading of favorite passages and a lack of knowledge of others. There is a difference, too, between casual reading and study.

Some workers like to study the Bible by topics. Daily reading may be centered around such topics as faith, love, family life, or any other subject in which the reader is interested. A topical concordance may be used to locate references on these subjects.

At other times the worker may prefer a book-by-book study. One pastor challenged his Sunday school workers to read the book of Ephesians every day for a month. Others may wish to read straight through the Bible, spending as much time as necessary to master the meaning of each chapter.

Character studies may be used as a basis for study. For example, a study could be made of the life of Samuel by reading all the references related to his life. Try writing the biography of the character after such a study.

Doctrinal studies are important for Beginner workers. We may not be teaching Baptist beliefs to our children, but we frequently encounter questions as we visit in the homes. "We are not church members, and we would like to know what Baptists believe," a mother may say to a teacher. She will have more confidence in the teacher who can answer such a question intelligently than in the one who must refer the mother to the pastor.

The Church Study Course for Teaching and Training contains many helpful books for the Bible student. Every Beginner worker should participate in the training program of the church.

2. *Of Child Growth and Development*

Another field in which Beginner workers must study is the field of child growth and development. There are many helpful books, magazines, and pamphlets on the market today. The Beginner worker who is growing in her knowledge of children is the worker who is studying constantly to learn what others are discovering through research and study.

Many newspapers feature regular columns on child care. One Beginner worker clips these articles and keeps them in an indexed notebook. Frequent reference is made to the notebook as problems are discussed in teachers' meeting or in visitation. Popular magazines often have regular articles of a similar nature.

Although few workers are financially able to buy all the books they need, church and public libraries usually have helps in child study. Librarians are glad to give assistance in locating references on a special problem.

Workers should read critically. They will not accept one writer as the final authority without studying other points of view. There are many books that are helpful in some areas, although parts of them may be controversial. For example, an excellent book on child guidance may have a chapter on religion which few Baptists would accept. Even though workers may not agree with all of the ideas presented in any book, their thinking will be stimulated and they will find value in reading.

3. *Of Special Subjects*

The third area in which workers need to study is related to special emphases and interests. Giving accurate and satisfactory answers to the child's questions is important. The nature materials are the basis for many questions, and there will be other areas from time to time which will demand research. One worker may be given the responsibility of finding sources of information about any such subject. These resources will be shared with other workers at teachers' meeting.

V. THE CHALLENGE TO SOUL-WINNING

Beginner workers should be soul-winners. We do not consider four- and five-year-olds as evangelistic prospects, but many of their parents are unsaved. Prospect visitation frequently takes us into homes where there are unsaved family members. Every department should have a prayer list of unsaved and unaffiliated parents.

Mr. Johnson was not a Christian and had no apparent interest in the church. His wife was a casual church member who did not take her religion very seriously. She did take Art, their only child, to Sunday school fairly regularly.

An Adult teacher had attempted unsuccessfully to interest Mr. Johnson in attending his class and in becoming a Christian. The pastor had talked with him on several occasions, but he had shown no interest.

When Art was promoted to the Beginner department, a worker visited in the home one evening when Mr. Johnson would be there. She found him eager to talk about Art and to hear the good things she had to tell about him. He was delighted that Art co-operated so well and that he showed initiative in activities.

"There's just one thing that bothers me when I think about Art," the worker said. "I do wish that you were a Christian and that Art could have a Christian home." They talked at length about the plan of salvation. The teacher had her Bible and they read several marked verses. Although he did not accept Christ that evening, the following Sunday Mr. Johnson made a profession of faith in the morning worship service.

Mr. Johnson said later that the teacher's interest in Art was the thing that won him. He felt (wrongly, more than likely) that the Adult teacher had visited him because he wanted his class to grow and that the pastor's primary interest had been in getting another church member. The teacher who was genuinely interested in his child could reach Mr. Johnson when no one else had been able to do so.

VI. The Challenge to Christlike Living

In no other area is Christlike living more important than with young children. We cannot hide our true selves from a little child.

Secret sins may be hidden from the children. Many things which we recognize as sins are things which children would not know about or understand.

Secret sins and a spirit-filled life do not go together, however, and even children can tell the difference in a life that is motivated by the Holy Spirit and one that is not. According to Galatians 5:22–23, "the fruit of the Spirit is love, joy, peace, longsuffering, gentleness, goodness, faith, meekness, temperance"—all qualities which will be seen by children if the worker is led by the Holy Spirit. Four- and five-year-olds do not know the meaning of these terms, but they are drawn to the teacher who has these characteristics.

The only idea many children have of Jesus is the picture they see portrayed in the lives of their teachers. "Jesus is like Mrs. Jones," the child from an unchristian home may be thinking. What kind of picture of Jesus is Mrs. Jones giving him? Does he think of Jesus as someone who is loving and forgiving or as someone who is impatient and irritable? Does his experience with Mrs. Jones make him want to know Jesus better?

Parents, too, expect their child's teachers to live Christlike lives. Even the parent who is unsaved expects his child's Sunday school teacher to be above reproach.

"Remember that we who are teachers will be judged by a much higher standard," is one translation of James 3:1.[2]

VII. THE REWARDS

Is it worth it? Teaching Beginners demands much in time and energy. Teachers must study and visit and attend meetings as well as work in the department on Sunday morning. Is it really worthwhile?

A Beginner worker thought so when she received a letter from Nancy's mother. The family had moved away and the worker had not seen them for several years when she received this letter.

"You will be glad to know that Nancy was baptized last night," she wrote. "I wanted you to know because you had so much to do with it."

The worker was puzzled. Nancy was only four years old when she was in her department. Both parents were devout Christians. Certainly the workers had not attempted to teach Nancy the plan of salvation.

And then she remembered that, as a result of an unpleasant Nursery experience, Nancy had cried every time she came near the church for more than a year. While she was in the four-year department the workers had, through love and understanding, helped her to solve her problem. Nancy grew to love Sunday school and to look forward to each ex-

---

[2] J. B. Phillips, *Letters to Young Churches* (New York: The Macmillan Co., 1953), p. 194. Used by permission.

perience in her Beginner room. Perhaps they had played a part in Nancy's accepting Christ when she was ten.

"Jesus is my very best friend," a teacher overheard one child say to another as they played together. She felt repaid for every hour she had spent in her Sunday school task!

"Thank you for what you have done for my son," a mother wrote the Beginner teachers. "Until we came here he always hated Sunday school, and we had to spank him every Sunday. He loved it from the first session here." Yes, it was worth the cost.

The chaplain of a federal penitentary spoke to a group of Sunday school workers in a state convention. "We don't have any children in our Sunday school," he told them. "But we have your failures; the ones you didn't reach."

One teacher in the audience thought of a Beginner child whose father had been sent to the penitentary for a horrible crime. Later, someone visited the family and invited them to Sunday school. The four-year-old was shy at first. Finally one day he arranged flowers, and later began to participate in other activities. If Sunday school could have any part in keeping that child from following in his father's way, it was worth every effort.

> I helped a little child to see
> That God had made a willow tree,
> And He became more real to me.
>
> I tried to lead a child through play
> To grow more Christ-like every day,
> And I myself became that way.
>
> I joined a junior child in prayer,
> And as we bowed in worship there
> I felt anew God's loving care.
>
> Lord, keep us ever quick to see
> By guiding children, we find thee.
>
> MABEL NIEDERMEYER [3]

FOR CLASS DISCUSSION

Make a list of the characteristics of the ideal Beginner worker. Which of these do you consider your strongest point? Which is your weakest? What practical plans can you make for improving in your weakest areas?

FOR FURTHER STUDY

Swor, Chester. *Very Truly Yours*. Nashville: Broadman Press, 1954.

Price, Eugenia. *Woman to Woman*. Grand Rapids: Zondervan, 1959.

Overstreet, Harry Allen. *The Mature Mind*. Sydney: Angus and Robertson, 1950.

Hudson, R. Loftin. *The Religion of a Mature Person*. Nashville: Broadman Press, 1952.

Burkhalter, Frank. *Living Abundantly*. Nashville: Convention Press, 1942.

Burroughs, P. E. *How to Win to Christ*. Nashville: Convention Press, 1934.

Hester, H. I. *The Book of Books*. Nashville: Convention Press, 1959.

Colson, Howard P. *Preparing to Teach the Bible*. Nashville: Convention Press, 1959.

Moore, H. Guy. *The Christian Life*. Nashville: Convention Press, 1961.

Teaching Suggestions

To MAKE the teaching of BIBLE TEACHING FOR FOUR'S AND FIVE'S effective, the teacher should study the entire book and the current issue of the *Beginner Teacher* before the first session. Additional references for further study may be found at the end of each chapter. Many of these books are available from public libraries.

Chapter 1

The motion pictures *Frustrating Four's and Fascinating Five's* or *Answering the Child's Why* may be used to enrich this session. They are available from your Baptist Book Store.

Chapter 2

If the class is composed of workers from one department only, consider a child in the department who has problems. Do the workers know the answers to all of the questions suggested on the Sunday School Information Sheet? What other information is needed? How can we help the child adjust to his problems?

If possible, ask one worker to arrange to spend an hour or two with that child before the next class session. She may take him to a playground, library, or to her own home, and report on the results at the next session.

The motion picture *When Should Grownups Help?* may be used during this session. The motion picture may be rented from New York University Film Library, 26 Washington Place, New York 3, New York.

Chapter 3

If an opaque projector is available, you may wish to project the objectives (a section at a time) on the screen for study. The teacher's concept of the entire program of religious education will be enriched by a study of all the objectives, especially the Nursery and Primary sections, as found in *The Curriculum Guide*.

Use a copy of *The Beginner Leader* for this session. Show how the Sunday school and Training Union monthly themes are related to each other and how they contribute toward the objectives for the Beginner years.

Chapter 4

If your department is not adequately equipped, you may wish to use portions of the filmstrip *Sunday Evening in a Beginner Department*. Although this filmstrip is prepared for Training Union workers, it pictures equipment which will be used for Beginners each time they come to church. It is available from your Baptist Book Store.

Order from your state Sunday school office the free diagrams for equipment for a Beginner department. As an outside project some members of the class might build needed equipment.

Ask class members to arrange a display of nature materials which may be used to help Beginners learn about God. If the class is large, four displays (living things, homes of animals, growing things, and products God provides) may be used.

If the class is advanced and has had a great deal of training and experience, *God's Wonders in Your Own Backyard, God's Wonders in Birds,* or *God's Wonders on the Farm* may be used. These motion pictures will help workers to understand how children may learn from nature.

Chapter 5

Evaluate a group of children's books (some good, some bad) using the principles suggested in this chapter.

Make finger paint (in the class) and let each worker experiment with using it.

Give each person in the class an opportunity to use modeling clay and to paint at the easel. If there is no easel available, one of the class projects might be the improvising of painting facilities.

Chapter 6

Look at the current issue of the *Beginner Teacher* and list the interwoven activities (songs, Bible verses, Bible activities, picture activities, games, etc.) suggested for one unit.

Chapter 7

As the teacher discusses routine guidance in the use of materials, she may wish to demonstrate (or have class members demonstrate) the following:

How to carry a watering can
How to wipe paint brushes
How to remove puzzle pieces
How to handle recordings

Chapter 8

Using a lesson from the current quarterly, let the class members plan a group time procedure for a department. With the teacher of the class (or someone she appoints) serving as the superintendent and the class members serving as Beginners, go through the group time session as you would on Sunday morning.

Chapter 9

The filmstrip, *First Steps in Religion,* may be used effectively during this session.

Chapter 10

A part of the closing period may be used for a dedication service. Class members may wish to share with others resolutions which they have made. Some may have prayer requests for their own lives. Close the class with a season of prayer.

For Review and Written Work

CHAPTER 1

1. What are some unwholesome influences in the lives of the Beginners in your community? Some wholesome influences?
2. Name some of the characteristics of Beginners.

CHAPTER 2

3. Name the basic needs of Beginners.
4. How can a Beginner teacher discover individual needs?

CHAPTER 3

5. How does a child learn "Be ye kind?"
6. How do we know when learning has taken place?

CHAPTER 4

7. What are some of the things a teacher can learn about children as she observes them working together?
8. Which of the nature materials mentioned in this chapter are available in your community? In what way could they be used to teach spiritual truths?

CHAPTER 5

9. What are some of the principles used in the selection of books for the bookrack?
10. What art materials are suggested for use with Beginners?
11. What are some of the values of using puzzles with Beginners?

CHAPTER 6

12. What interwoven activities may be used during activity time?
13. Give an example of ways in which one of these might be used.
14. What are the two dangers in the use of interwoven activities? Discuss.

CHAPTER 7

15. How can a teacher help when children are not working together well?
16. Select any two of the materials mentioned in this chapter and give some general rules for their use.
17. What should a teacher do when a child does not wish to take part in any activity?

CHAPTER 8

18. Name some of the elements of group time.
19. What should be considered in the choice of songs for group time?
20. Give suggestions for effective storytelling.

CHAPTER 9

21. Why is it important that parents and teachers share their goals?
22. What are some of the ways parents and teachers can help each other if they have shared problems?
23. How can teachers encourage the use of *Home Life* in the homes?

CHAPTER 10

24. What traits do you consider important for Beginner workers?
25. In what three areas should Beginner workers study?
26. What different plans of systematic Bible study are suggested in this chapter?